# SPIRITUAL WARFARE

## QUIMBANDA SPELLS & RITUALS TO DEFEAT THE ENEMY

***CARLOS ANTONIO DE BOURBON-GALDIANO-MONTENEGRO***

**AMERICAN CANDOMBLE CHURCH PUBLICATIONS, LOS ANGELES, CALIFORNIA**

# SPIRITUAL WARFARE

QUIMBANDA SPELLS & RITUALS TO DEFEAT THE ENEMY



**AMERICAN CANDOMBLE CHURCH PUBLICATIONS**

**P.O. BOX 881377**

**LOS ANGELES, CALIFORNIA 90009**

**LEGAL DISCLAIMER**

*No part of this book may be reproduced in any manner without written permission from the publisher or the author of this book. This book contains formulas that were used in the historical AFRO-BRAZILIAN religious practices of Quimbanda, Candomble, Macumba and Umbanda. The author and the publisher do not encourage any of the practices in this book nor do we assume any liabilities for presenting those formulas or any information in this book. The formulas are presented for curious only. Neither the author, Carlos Antonio De Bourbon-Galdiano-Montenegro nor the publisher, American Candomble Church assumes any responsibilities for the outcome of any of the spells, rituals or initiations in this book. We make no claims to any supernatural powers of these traditional initiation rituals. All inquiries or comments may be directed to the publisher. You must be at least 18 years of age or older to purchase this book or to purchase any of the supplies listed herein.*

**TABLE OF CONTENTS**

*A DIAGRAM PICTURE SHOWING THE FERRAMENTA OF KING EXU REI.*

# INTRODUCTION

The best part about spiritual war is "revenge". All of the following Afro-Brazilian Quimbanda spells and rituals are real and authentic. I have personally used all of them over the past years to defeat and triumph over my occult enemies. All of the following spells and rituals should be followed exactly as they are presented here in this book if you want to see fast magical results and success. I hope that you enjoy them as I have over the past years of working in the world of Afro-Brazilian black magic in the "world of colored darkness". Lately, I have received a number of requests asking for help and guidance in relation to psychic or spiritual attacks. When I start to receive multiple requests on the same subject, it is time to write up what I know so that I can, I hope, help as many people as possible.

**SARAVA**

*Carlos Antonio De Bourbon-Galdiano-Montenegro*

March 31, 2011

*A DIAGRAM PICTURE SHOWING THE FERRAMENTA OF QUEEN MARIA PADILLA REINA.*

## THE SEVEN QUIMBANDA PRINCIPLES OF SPIRITUAL WAR

The following rules of engagement of spiritual war are known as "***THE SEVEN QUIMBANDA PRINCIPLES OF SPIRITUAL WAR***". Before beginning any type of spiritual war it is important that you read all of the following spiritual recommendations. If you follow all of the following spiritual recommendations you will always triumph over your occult enemies. The most important factor about engaging in a spiritual war is that it is time consuming and many of times require lots of money to purchase magical supplies. Spiritual war also requires that the individual medium or spiritualists that will be leading the war against their enemies be a powerful medium with clear body, mind and soul.

## ***NEVER ATTACK YOUR ENEMY FIRST***

In the art of spiritual war you should always be prepared for an attack from your occult enemies, but you should never attack first. Always let your enemy's attack you first and then spiritually access the situation and then go from there. Because of the Quimbanda spiritual law of "*Divine Justice*" we believe that if you allow your enemy to attack first you will be able to attack them without receiving any Karmic retributions whatsoever because the spirit Exu says, "that it is right and it is just." If you allow your occult enemies to attack first, the battle is already half way won in your favor.

## ***ALWAYS CONSULT WITH THE SPIRITS FIRST THROUGH DIVINATION BEFORE PROCEEDING***

In the art of spiritual war you should always consult with the Quimbanda spirits first before embarking on any type of spiritual attack against your enemies. This can be done using the Quimbanda Chamalongo Divination 16 Shell method sacred to the Spirit Exu, or through the traditional four (4) coconut shell Chamalongo Divination method, or through using a Quimbanda Scrying Mirror to see exactly what your enemies are doing. Throughout the entire time of the spiritual war, divinations must be constantly done in order to see what your enemies are plotting and planning. Spiritual consultations are also necessary to find out what kind of spiritual recommendations and spiritual offerings that are required by the spirits before embarking on any type of spiritual battle against your enemies.

*MAKE SURE THAT THE SPIRITS OF YOUR TEMPLE ARE APPEASED AND RITUALLY FED BEFORE ANY TYPE OF SPIRITUAL WAR.*

## ATTACK YOUR ENEMY FIRST WHERE THEY ARE MOST VULNERABLE

Always attack your occult enemies where they are most vulnerable.

"*REMEMBER IN THE ART OF WAR EVERYTHING AND EVERYBODY IS FAIR GAME & A TARGET*" - THAT'S JUST HOW IT IS.

## ***ATTACK YOUR ENEMY WITH BLINDING SPEED***

Speed is the essence of spiritual war. Take advantage of the enemy's unpreparedness. Spiritually attack them and strike him where he has taken no precautions. To move with such speed does not mean to do things hastily. In reality, speed requires much preparation. Reducing the time it takes to make decisions, develop new spiritual weapons, implement strategies and respond to the enemy's moves is crucial. To think through and understand the opponent's reaction to one's possible moves also is essential.

## ***ALWAYS USE STRATEGIC AND STRUCTURED PLANNING***

Plan your spiritual attack strategically using deception and structured planning. Don't stop attacking your enemy until you render them spiritually disabled. One must be able to "shape" the enemy. Therefore those skilled in the art of spiritual war bring the enemy to the field of battle and are not brought there by him. To achieve everything discussed so far takes a special kind of leader; one who can see the correct course of action and take it immediately, who can relate to the members of your temple.

## ***DON'T STOP UNTIL YOU RENDER YOUR ENEMY SPIRITUALLY DISABLED***

Shaping the enemy means changing the rules of the contest and making one's opponent conform to one's desires and actions. It means taking control of the situation away from the enemy and putting it into one's own hands. One way of shaping the enemy is by the skillful use of alliances. By building a strong web of alliances, the moves of the opponent can be limited. Also, by eliminating its alliances, one can weaken the enemy. Look into the matter of his alliances and cause them to be severed and dissolved. If an enemy has alliances, the problem is grave and the enemy's position strong; if he has no alliances the problem is minor and the enemy's position weak.

## ***PRACTICE THE SPIRITUAL LAW OF DIRECT & INDIRECT***

By keeping plans and strategy closely held and using tactics to deceive the enemy about one's true intentions, one can continue to shape them by employing direct and indirect approaches. He who knows the art of the direct and the indirect approach will be victorious. A direct attack is one that occurs in an expected place at an expected time. An indirect assault is one that comes as a surprise, both in location and timing. By combining direct attacks on the enemy to fix their leaders' attention and deceive them, one can then use indirect attacks to win complete victory. By utilizing the indirect and direct approaches and skillfully crafting alliances the opponent can be put on the defensive and made more vulnerable to future attacks.

## HOW TO DETERMINE IF YOU HAVE BEEN SPIRITUALLY ATTACKED

Unless you are as experienced and seasoned as I am in the "Art of Spiritual War," psychic or spiritual attacks aren't always easy to spot. For some people, the attacks are so subtle, or have been going on for so long, that the person isn't aware of the attack. The more obvious and overt spiritual attacks will be left at your front door in the form of a bundled package, sprinkled dirt, scattered oils on your front porch & door knob, a dead chicken or animal.

**Here is a list of some more symptoms of a spiritual attack**

- *Your candles on your spiritual altar are burning black.*

- *The candles on your spiritual altar explode or the glass cracks.*

- *You start to dream about your enemies.*

- *You start to have conflict with people around you for no apparent reason.*

- *Individuals around you start to have conflict with you for no apparent reason.*

- *You start to have problems at your job for no apparent reason.*

- *You lose your job for no apparent reason.*

- *People don't want to be around you.*

- *You start to have constant legal problems or problems with the police.*

- *You start to have nightmares.*

- *You start to feel sick.*

- *The doctors can't find out what is wrong with you.*

- *You start to feel depressed.*

- *You start to have low self- esteem about yourself.*

- *You are constantly involved in accidents of any kind.*

- *You feel suicidal.*

*- You lose your job for no apparent reason.*

*- People start to become hostile towards you.*

*- You start to have irrational fears.*

*- You start to have panic attacks.*

*- You start to have phobias.*

*- You start to have addictive behavior.*

*- You start to have visible bruises on your body.*

*- Your mate leaves you.*

*- You leave start to fight with or just leave your mate for no apparent reason.*

*- You start to have abnormal medical problems.*

*- You start to have seizures, pain, blackouts, sudden severe headaches, numbness in arms or legs, temporary paralysis, stomach aches and asthma attacks.*

*- You start to hear buzzing in your ears.*

*- You start to feel extremely hot or cold.*

*- You hear voices of people that you can't see or that are not there.*

*- You feel an invisible unseen presence around you.*

*- You feel an invisible unseen presence get on top of you at night and hold's your mouth shut.*

*- You see shadows of figures and unseen people in and around your house.*

*- Things start getting moved and misplaced in your house.*

*- Your animals, birds or fish start to die mysteriously.*

*- Animals start to fear you or get aggressive with you for no apparent reason.*

**THERE ARE MANY MORE SYMPTOMS OF A SPIRITUAL ATTACK, BUT THESE ARE THE MOST COMMON.**

It would be my advice that if you are not experienced in the realm of black magic and the "art of spiritual warfare" that you seek out the spiritual advice of a qualified Quimbandeiro Priest.

## HOW TO PROTECT THE FOUR (4) CORNERS OF THE OUTSIDE OF YOUR HOUSE

It is a common mistake among individuals to leave their homes vulnerable to spiritual attacks. By doing the following spiritual ritual you will be able to protect any type of negative energy from crossing over and onto your property. The following is a simple method that is used by initiates of the Quimbanda religion to protect their properties against witchcraft attacks. Although it requires that certain items be buried outside at each one of the four (4) corners it can however be done by burying the items in a large flower pot that can be covered over by the following distinct dirt and then a plant is planted in the center of the flower pot. The type of magical plant that should be planted is called in Portuguese, "**Espada De São Jorge**". Or in English, the "**Sword of Saint George**" plant. This very hardy indoor and outdoor plant is very popular and can be found at most well stocked garden centers or Botanicas. The scientific name is called, **Sansevieria trifasciata** is a species of Sansevieria, native to tropical West Africa from Nigeria east to the Democratic Republic of the Congo. It is an evergreen herbaceous perennial plant forming dense stands, spreading by way of its creeping rhizome, which is sometimes above ground, sometimes underground. Its stiff leaves grow vertically from a basal rosette. Mature leaves are dark green with light gray-green cross-banding and usually range between 70-90 cm in length and 5-6 cm in width. It is commonly called the snake plant because of the shape of its leaves, or mother-in-law's tongue because of their sharpness. In Japan it is also called "**Tiger's Tail**." In Brazil it is commonly known as **Espada De São Jorge** (Sword of Saint George). Due to its bladelike shape, it is commonly associated with Ogun, the Orixa of war (usually associated with Saint George), and is used in rituals to remove the evil eye. In the Quimbanda religion this spirit is known by the name of **Mukumbe**. A yellow-tipped variant is known as "**Espada De Santa Barbara**" (Sword of Saint Barbara), and is associated with Iansan/Oya, the female Orixa of storms (usually associated with the sword-bearing image of Saint Barbara). In Africa as well as in Latin America, the plant is used as a protective charm against evil or bewitchment. Although the following formula is traditionally used outside your home at the four corners, it can also be done inside of a flower pot and placed at either side of your front and back doors to your house and even at the four corners of the inside of your house.

***THE FOLLOWING QUIMBANDA FORMULA CAN ALSO BE USED TO PROTECT YOUR HOUSE FROM ENVIOUS INDIVIDUALS, BURGLERS AND FROM THE POLICE FROM COMING INTO YOUR HOME.***

**Sansevieria trifasciata**, *The Sword of St. George*.

**HOW TO PREPARE THE SWORD OF SAINT GEORGE (MUKOMBE) PLANT FOR THE FOUR CORNERS**

This ritual should be started on a Friday at 12 midnight.

**ITEMS NEEDED**

- A well rooted Sword of Saint George Plant
- A large flower pot
- A small metal sword or new knife
- One small quartz crystal
- One stone from a railroad crossing
- Coins from 7 different countries from around the world
- Twenty-one peonia seeds
- The metal tools (ferramentas) of the Orixa Ogun
- Three used railroad spikes
- Palm oil (Dende)
- Dirt from 7 crossroads
- Dirt from 7 churches
- Dirt from a hospital
- Dirt from the railroad tracks
- Dirt from a jail
- Dirt from a courthouse
- Dirt from a police station
- Dirt from a bank
- Dirt from a mountain
- Crushed glass
- Mouse trap
- Twenty-one rusty nails
- Pemba powder (cascarilla/eggshell powder)
- One rattlesnake rattle
- Red paint
- Beef blood (you can purchase this from any butcher meat market)
- Red candles

## HOW TO PREPARE THE PROTECTION RITUAL

- Paint the Quimbanda Spirit Signature of **MUKOMBE** at the bottom of the flower pot using the red paint and allow it to dry.

- After the paint has dried, do the following.

- In a large mixing bowl add all of the following ingredients: Dirt from 7 crossroads, Dirt from 7 churches, Dirt from a hospital, Dirt from the railroad tracks, Dirt from a jail, Dirt from a courthouse, Dirt from a police station, Dirt from a bank, Dirt from a mountain and the Pemba powder (cascarilla/eggshell powder). Mix well.

- Next add all of the following dried herbs in powdered form to the above mixed dirts: Rue, Basil, Rosemary, Crushed Dragon's Blood Powder and Bay Leaf. Mix well.

- Next add a generous amount of fresh beef blood and a small amount of palm oil to the above mixture. Mix well.

- Next add a small amount of the above mixture to the bottom of the flower pot.

- Next place all of the following items into the flower pot: A small metal sword or new knife, One small quartz crystal, One stone from a railroad crossing, Coins from 7 different countries from around the world, Twenty-one peonia seeds, The metal tools (ferramentas) of the Orixa Oggun, Three used railroad spikes, Crushed glass, mouse trap, Twenty-one rusty nails and One rattlesnake rattle. The iron metal tools (ferramentas) of the Orixa Oggun and the railroad spikes should be placed in good positions into the flower pot.

- Next place some more of the moist dirt mixture into the flower pot directly on top of all of the above items.

- Next place the Sword of St. George Plant into the center of the flower pot and then cover the roots and the base of the plant all the way to the top of the flower pot to firmly anchor the plant into the flower pot.

- Next place the plant(s) in the desired location and water them generously using Holy Water from a Catholic Church.

- Next light a red candle next to each of the plants and say the following prayer to Saint George in front of each of the potted plants.

## SPIRITUAL INSTRUCTIONS

- Pray the following prayer for nine consecutive Fridays at 12 midnight in front of a red candle.

- Give your plants Holy Water from a Catholic Church for nine consecutive Fridays at 12 midnight.

- Give and feed your plants beefs blood once a year.

- Place an image picture or statue of Saint George in your home with a red candle burning in front of it always.

## A PRAYER TO THE MOST GLORIOUS SAINT GEORGE

*In the name of Nzambi and the Quimbanda Trinity. SARAVA*

*O Glorious Warrior, servant of Nzambi, Saint George. I invoke thee to protect me against my enemies known and unknown. SARAVA*

*O Glorious Warrior, servant of the Quimbanda Trinity, Saint George. I invoke thee to place a protective light around me, my family and my home so that my enemies will not see nor hear this ritual of divine protection. SARAVA*

*O Glorious Warrior Saint George cover my body in your protective armor so that no harm or danger will cross over my path. SARAVA*

*O Glorious Warrior Saint George just as you slayed the dragon so shall you slay my enemies. SARAVA*

*O Glorious Warrior Saint George protect and deliver me from my enemies, from all harm, from all witchcraft and from all tragedy. SARAVA*

*O Glorious Warrior Saint George, I beseech you and feel confident that I will be satisfied, at this difficult time of my life, in the name of Nzambi and the Quimbanda Trinity, with Your Divine Sword fight, will cut all evil away from my path. SARAVA*

*O Glorious Warrior Saint George With the strength of thy power, I cover myself in the protection of your shield, to fight the good against all evil or negative influence that is in my path. SARAVA*

*Glorious Saint George, on behalf of Nzambi and the Quimbanda Trinity extend me your shield and its powerful weapons, defending me with your strength and your greatness, and that under the legs of your faithful horse my enemies are humble and submissive to you. SARAVA*

*O Glorious Warrior Saint George, just as you did slay the fierce Dragon, come to my aid and protect me from all temptations of the evil, dangers, difficulties and sufferings. SARAVA*

*O Glorious Warrior Saint George cover me with your blanket, hiding me from my enemies and my persecutors. SARAVA*

*O Glorious Warrior Saint George cover me in your cloak so I will be invisible to my enemies. SARAVA*

*O Glorious Warrior Saint George under your protection, may I never be harmed by my enemies nor may my blood never run in the streets from any accidents or tragedies caused by my enemies. SARAVA*

*O Glorious Warrior Saint George, by your ways, by your virtues, through your faith, come to my aid and proclaim the presence of Nzambi and the Quimbanda Trinity. (Make the request here). SARAVA*

***A PICTURE OF THE MOST GLORIOUS SAINT GEORGE.***

## HOW TO CLEANSE YOUR HOUSE AFTER A SPIRITUAL ATTACK

This is a two (2) part ritual. The first part of the ritual requires that you make and prepare a very strong spiritual floor wash to spray or mop the inside of your house. The same floor wash will also be used to dress your yard or to sprinkle around the outside four corners of your property. The second part of this ritual requires you to make and prepare powerful Quimbanda incense to burn around your house as well as outside your house to complete the ritual. This ritual also requires that you prepare a special Quimbanda 9 day cleansing candle ritual.

*This cleansing ritual should be started at 12 Midnight on a Monday, Friday or Saturday.*

### ITEMS REQUIRED

- *One brass bell*
- *Quimbanda Ritual Floor Wash*
- *Quimbanda Ritual Cleansing Incense*
- *Various items for the 9 Day Candle Ritual*
- *Quimbanda Ritual Prayer of Exu*

## HOW TO MAKE QUIMBANDA RITUAL FLOOR WASH

Mix all of the following ingredients together and place into a large bottle until ready to use for the cleansing ritual.

- *Holy Water*

- *Ammonia*

- *Brazilian Quimbanda Spiritual Cologne / Eau De Portugal Cologne*

## HOW TO MAKE BRAZILIAN QUIMBANDA SPIRITUAL COLOGNE (EAU DE PORTUGAL COLOGNE)

Mix 7 drops each from all of the following fragrance/essential oils together with one cup of Vodka and place into a large bottle and place in a dark location for 24 hours before using or until ready to mix into the Quimbanda Ritual Floor Wash. This particular formula of Brazilian Quimbanda Spiritual Cologne can also be used in a spray bottle to spray around the house occasionally when you feel like there is negative energy in and around your house. (Eau De Portugal Cologne).

- ***BERGAMOT*** - fragrance oil
- ***LAVENDAR*** - fragrance oil
- ***ORANGE*** - fragrance oil
- ***NEROLI*** - fragrance oil
- ***ROSEMARY*** - fragrance oil
- ***CLOVE*** - fragrance oil
- ***CLARY SAGE*** - fragrance oil
- ***PATCHOULI*** - fragrance oil

## HOW TO MAKE QUIMBANDA RITUAL CLEANSING INCENSE (DEFUMADORES)

Mix all of the following ingredients together and place into jar until ready to use for the cleansing ritual. This particular Quimbanda Ritual Cleansing Incense must be burned on top of hot incense charcoals. When burning incense on hot charcoals they must be burned in a metal pan. Do not burn in a ceramic or plastic dish because it will catch fire.

- *Dragons Blood Powder*
- *Camphor Chunks Powder*
- *Resin Church Incense Powder*
- *Rosemary Powder*
- *Lavender Powder*
- *Clove Powder*
- *Cedar Wood Powder*
- *Bay Leaf Powder*

## HOW TO PREPARE THE QUIMBANDA 9 DAY CANDLE CLEANSING SPELL

- *One clear drinking glass*
- *Holy Water*
- *One green lime*
- *Kosher rock salt*
- *Nine (9) Red small (4 - 6 inch) stick candles*
- *One white ceramic plate*

### PREPARATION

- Cut a lime in the form of a cross and place it into a clear drinking glass. Make sure to not completely pull the lime apart.

- Add the Holy Water to the glass cup.

- Mix the Kosher Rock Salt into the Holy water into the glass cup.
- Add the lime to the liquid mixture into the glass cup.
- Place a small white ceramic plate over the top of the glass cup.
- Make sure that the liquid of the glass cup comes all the way to the top rim of the cup.
- Flip the glass and the plate over. Do not allow the water to come out.
- Place a red candle on top of the glass and light it.
- Place one red candle each night at 12 Midnight for nine (9) consecutive nights.

## RITUAL PRAYER TO EXU TO CLEANSE YOUR HOUSE AFTER A SPIRITUAL ATTACK

*In the name of Nzambi, the Lord of Heaven - SARAVA*

*In the name of the Quimbanda Trinity, who govern the Heavens and the Earth - SARAVA*

*Exu by the Divine Sword of the King of Kings, I lay down my enemies at your feet- SARAVA*

*Exu by the Divine Sword of the King of Kings, I do bind my enemies in thy most sacred name- SARAVA*

*Exu by the Divine Sword of the King of Kings, I do blind my enemies in thy most sacred name- SARAVA*

*Exu by the Divine Sword of the King of Kings, I do destroy my enemies in thy most sacred name- SARAVA*

*Exu by the Divine Sword of the King of Kings, Give me victory to triumph over my enemies- SARAVA*

*Exu by the Divine Sword of the King of Kings, Give me victory to defeat my enemies- SARAVA*

*Exu by the Divine Sword of the King of Kings, I wash my hands clean like Pontius Pilate- SARAVA*

## THE HOUSE CLEANSING RITUAL

The Quimbanda House Cleansing Ritual creates a completely cleansed and spiritually positive atmosphere by purifying the home from any negative energy.

STEP ONE

Place the glass with the lime on a flat table surface into the center of the spirit signature of the Quimbanda Cross. After you have placed the filled glass with the liquids into the center of the Quimbanda Cross then light the first red candle and say - SARAVA.

STEP TWO

Light the Quimbanda Ritual Incense and allow the smoke to permeate the entire house. Take the incense and pass it around the entire house beginning at the area furthest from the front door.

STEP THREE

Place the Quimbanda Ritual Floor Wash in a spray bottle and start to spray every room of the house with it.

STEP FOUR

Facing the East start to ring the brass bell in your right hand and say the following:

*IN THE NAME OF NZAMBI, GOD OF HEAVEN AND EARTH – SARAVA*

Turn and then face the West and while ringing the brass bell in your right hand and say the following:

*IN THE NAME OF EXU MAIORAL, KING OF THE ASTRAL WORLD – SARAVA*

Facing the South start to ring the brass bell in your right hand and say the following:

*IN THE NAME OF EXU REI, KING OF THE SEVEN KINGDOMS – SARAVA*

Facing the North start to ring the brass bell in your right hand and say the following:

*IN THE NAME OF MARIA PADILLA REINA, QUEEN OF THE SEVEN KINGDOMS – SARAVA*

STEP FIVE

After you have formally saluted the Quimbanda spirits of the four (4) corners then go to the front door and while ringing the brass bell in your right hand say the following prayer:

*In the name of Nzambi, the Lord of Heaven - SARAVA*
*In the name of the Quimbanda Trinity, who govern the Heavens and the Earth - SARAVA*
*Exu by the Divine Sword of the King of Kings, I lay down my enemies at your feet- SARAVA*
*Exu by the Divine Sword of the King of Kings, I do bind my enemies in thy most sacred name- SARAVA*
*Exu by the Divine Sword of the King of Kings, I do blind my enemies in thy most sacred name- SARAVA*
*Exu by the Divine Sword of the King of Kings, I do destroy my enemies in thy most sacred name- SARAVA*
*Exu by the Divine Sword of the King of Kings, Give me victory to triumph over my enemies- SARAVA*
*Exu by the Divine Sword of the King of Kings, Give me victory to defeat my enemies- SARAVA*
*Exu by the Divine Sword of the King of Kings, I wash my hands clean like Pontius Pilate- SARAVA*

STEP SIX

After reciting the above prayer to the spirit Exu, start to walk through the entire front yard while ringing the bell while speaking your intentions aloud. After walking thoroughly the entire yard with the bell, then start to pour generous amounts of the Quimbanda Ritual Floor Wash at the four corners of your front yard and also at the outside four corners of your house.

STEP SEVEN

Allow the incense to completely finish burning and the fumes to diminish completely before reentering into your house. Once inside the house then once again start to ring the brass bell and walk around the entire house and every room. When you have completed this step then take a Quimbanda Spiritual Cleansing Bath. The Quimbanda Spiritual Cleansing Bath should be taken for nine (9) consecutive nights before going to bed.

STEP EIGHT

Light one new red candle on top of the glass containing the liquid and the the lime for nine (9) consecutive nights at 12 midnight. Each night that you place a new red candle and light it, recite the *RITUAL PRAYER TO EXU TO CLEANSE YOUR HOUSE AFTER A SPIRITUAL ATTACK* and walk around the house while ringing the bell.

*THIS VERY POWERFUL BRAZILIAN QUIMBANDA CLEANSING RITUAL WILL REMOVE AND BANISH ALL WITCHCRAFT, EVIL SPIRITS AND NEGATIVE ENERGY.*

**THIS RITUAL CAN ONLY BE PERFORMED ONCE A MONTH**

## THE QUIMBANDA MAGIC MIRROR

The Quimbanda Magic Mirror is a scrying mirror that can be used to see the movements of your enemies and to spy on them. If you are an experienced initiate of any Congo religious tradition you can prepare your own. Once it is prepared correctly you will be able to use it as a powerful weapon against your enemies to know exactly what, how and when your enemies are plotting against you. The Quimbanda Magic Mirror should always be kept on your Quimbanda spiritual altar and covered at all times until ready to invoke the mysteries of the sacred oracle. The entire ritual to prepare the authentic original Quimbanda Magic Mirror is available in the book written by Carlos Antonio De Bourbon-Galdiano-Montenegro, ***MAGIC MIRROR, THE SACRED QUIMBANDA ORACLE OF EXU.***

## HOW TO INTERPRET THE BURNING OF CANDLES IN SPIRITUAL WAR

The interpretation or reading candles burning on your spiritual altar is an important factor when trying to determine the vibration of energy in your home. By reading the candles as they burn, you will be able to determine if the energy in your home is spiritually clean or if it may have negativity coming to it from a negative source. When you are in a spiritual war, it is important to pay close attention to how your candles are burning so you will be able to determine how to magically approach the situation. The following is a list of some of the most common candle burning interpretations on how to accurately read your candles. There are many more, but these are the most common.

### WHAT IF THE CANDLE EXPLOADS WHILE IT IS BURING?

This usually refers to candles that are housed in glass jars or containers, but I have also seen pillar candles explode. There are two different ways to interpret this. If it is a protection or reversing candle it means that the candle protected something from attacking you and/or a lot of negative energy has been directed towards you. If the candle is being used to dominate or cause conflict to someone, it means that the person is being protected spiritually. If this is the case, you are to light another candle of the same type to break their protection to allow the spell to work correctly.

### WHAT IF I LIGHT A CANDLE AND THE WICK DOES NOT WANT TO BURN?

If the candle is a prosperity or protection candle, this means that other type of spiritual cleansing must be done before the beginning of this spell to remove the negativity of the environment before proceeding. If the candle is being used for domination of to inflict harm then another type of spell must be used.

**WHAT DOES IT MEAN WHEN AFTER I LIGHT THE CANDLE THE FLAME IS EXTREMELY HIGH?**

The spell is going to be effective and work fast. If for prosperity or protection, the environment is clear of negativity. If for domination and harm, you will most likely see quick results as they do not have spiritual protection.

**WHAT DOES IT MEAN WHEN AFTER I LIGHT THE CANDLE THE FLAME IS LOW OR VERY WEAK?**

In regards to prosperity & luck, cleanse your environment. In regards to domination and harm, they are resisting due to a strong spirit and it will be awhile before you see results. It is suggested that you try another spell in combination with the present one to see faster results.

**WHAT IF I LIGHT A CANDLE AND THE GLASS TURNS COMPLETELY BLACK?**

If after the candle burns down the entire glass is black, it is thought to mean that negativity or witchcraft has been directed towards you. Cleansing your environment and lighting a reversing candle should do the trick. If this happens when burning a candle to dominate or harm someone they suggest stopping because it may possibly turned back on you.

**WHAT IF I LIGHT A CANDLE AND THE TOP HALF OF THE GLASS TURNS COMPLETELY BLACK?**

If only the top part of the glass burns black this means that the spell was initially met with negativity before it began to work.

**WHAT IF I LIGHT A CANDLE AND ONLY THE BOTTOM HALF OF THE GLASS TURNS COMPLETELY BLACK?**
If it is a candle for prosperity or luck, negativity was sent your way and the candle detected it. If used to dominate or harm, the spirit of the person was alerted and reversed the spell.

**WHAT IF I LIGHT A CANDLE AND THE WAX BURNS ONLY ON ONE SIDE?**
This means that the spell will only be part way effective. This means that the wrong candle or candle dressing was used.

**WHAT IF I LIGHT A CANDLE AND THE GLASS CRACKS?**
If being used for self-protection, this means that the candle broke the negativity in the environment. This can also mean witchcraft or the presence of secret enemies. If being used to dominate, it means the protection of the individual was broken.

**WHAT IF I LIGHT A CANDLE AND THE FLAME CRACKLES?**
If for self-protection it means that someone is talking about you and has bad intentions directed towards you. If being used to harm, it means the individual is thinking about you.

**WHAT IF I LIGHT A CANDLE AND IT HAS TWO FLAMES BURNING FROM THE WICK?**
The center or main flame represents you. If being used for protection each one other than the center one represents an enemy. If being used to dominate, it means that the person is being helped by other people.

**WHAT IF I LIGHT A CANDLE AND IT HAS THREE FLAMES BURNING FROM THE WICK?**
This could represent three enemies or even a third person trying to cause problems between you and your mate.

**WHAT IF I LIGHT A CANDLE AND THE FLAME STARTS TO FLICKER OR MOTION FROM SIDE TO SIDE?**
When a candle flame flickers, this signifies the presence of spirits. Usually it means good spirits or the presence of your spirit guides assisting you.

**WHAT IF I LIGHT A CANDLE AND THE ENTIRE TOP OF THE CANDLE INCLUDING THE WICK CATCH FIRE?**
This means that the spell is being fought off by guardian spirits but more than likely, the spell will be successful.

**WHAT IF I LIGHT A CANDLE AND THE CANDLE FLAME KEEPS TURNING OFF?**
If the spell is for protection this means that while the job was being performed, witchcraft was directed your way and your spirits were unable to fight it off. If directed towards another, their spirits were able to fight the attack off & have alarmed the individual. Another type of spell must be performed.

**CAN A CANDLE BE EXTINGUISHED AND THEN LIGHTED AGAIN AT A LATER TIME?**
Only a candle being used to bring prosperity or success to an individual may be extinguished before it has completely burned. If being used to dominate or harm someone, the candle flame must never be put out or the spell will not work. The guardian spirits of the other individual will then have time to prepare and reverse it back on to you.

**WHAT IS THE CORRECT WAY TO PUT A CANDLE FLAME OUT?**
Placing a plate over the flame thus allowing the flame to extinguish itself naturally or use a candle snuffer.

**WHAT IF I EXTINGUISH A CANDLE FLAME AND IT THEN RELIGHTS ITSELF?**
This means that your guardian spirits do not want you to turn the candle off because they are detecting something good or bad for you. If the candle is turned off they cannot assist you effectively.

**WHAT IF A SEVEN (7) DAY RELIGIOUS GLASS CANDLE BURNS OUT BEFORE THE 7TH DAY?**
This means that the spell is working fast and another candle must be lit immediately. Money is coming in regards to prosperity spells, a lot of negativity in regards to reversing spells and in spells of harm, that the individual's spirit is fighting it off but it will soon be successful.

## CEREMONIAL ALTARS OF THE QUIMBANDA TRINITY

Ritually preparing the altar of the Quimbanda Trinity is an important aspect of performing this very powerful ritual. I have provided in the following pages various examples of how to correctly prepare an altar for the spirits of the Quimbanda Trinity. All Quimbanda altars should be set up facing the direction of the East. Altars can be set up in outside garden patios, balconies or in a designated ritual temple area in your home. Altars can also be temporaily set up for the purpose of performing this sacred ritual in remote locations such as the forest, fields, mountain, near the rivers or beaches. In the Quimbanda magico-religious tradition, having an altar set up in your temple or home is mandatory. An altar is any structure upon which offerings such as sacrifices and votive offerings are made for religious purposes, or some other sacred place where ceremonies take place. Altars are usually found at shrines, and they can be located in temples, churches and other places of worship. If you will be using the spells and sacred rituals from this book and from any other of my books written about the Quimbanda religious tradition you will need to first prepare an altar to their mysteries.

## HOW TO PREPARE A SPIRITUAL BATH FOR SPIRITUAL BATTLE
(BANHO DE GUERRA)

The following Brazilian Quimbanda Spiritual Bath should be taken before you begin any ritual of spiritual war against your enemies. This particular spiritual bath will cleanse your aura and reinforce it with supernatural powers of protection. By taking this spiritual bath you will also be ensured that your powers will be maximized and allow you to focus on your rituals of spiritual battle. This bath should be taken before beginning each and every ritual before raging war against your enemies known and unknown.

### INGREDIENTS

*Fresh Leafs from a Brazilian Pepper Tree*
*Fresh Bay Leafs*
*Fresh Rosemary leafs*
*Brazilian Spiritual Cologne (Eau De Portugal Cologne)*
*Brazilian Quimbanda Ritual Black Soap*

### RITUAL INSTRUCTIONS

Boil all of the following ingredients in a large metal pot until the liquid is dark; Fresh Leafs from a Brazilian Pepper Tree, Fresh Bay Leafs and the Fresh Rosemary leafs. After the liquid has cooled, strain the liquid into a bucket and add the Brazilian Spiritual Cologne (Eau De Portugal Cologne) to it. Mix the liquid bath well. Take a spiritual bath using the liquid and wash your entire body, including your head. Use the Brazilian Quimbanda Ritual Black Soap while taking your spiritual bath.

## HOW TO PREPARE A SPIRITUAL CLEANSING BATH
(BANHO DE DESCARGA)

The following Brazilian Quimbanda Spiritual Cleansing Bath should be taken when you feel that you have been spiritually attacked by your enemies. It should also be taken after every magical ritual that you wage spiritual war against your enemies so that the negative vibration that you may attract to your aura will be cleansed and you will be spiritually clean and free from harm and negative vibration.

INGREDIENTS

*Fresh Leafs from a Lemon or Lime Tree*
*Fresh Basil Leafs*
*Fresh Rue leafs*
*Brazilian Spiritual Cologne (Eau De Portugal Cologne)*
*Brazilian Quimbanda Ritual Black Soap*

RITUAL INSTRUCTIONS

Boil all of the following ingredients in a large metal pot until the liquid is dark; Fresh Leafs from a Lemon or Lime Tree, Fresh Basil Leafs, Fresh Rue leafs. After the liquid has cooled, strain the liquid into a bucket and add the Brazilian Spiritual Cologne (Eau De Portugal Cologne) to it. Mix the liquid bath well. Take a spiritual bath using the liquid and wash your entire body, including your head. Use the Brazilian Quimbanda Ritual Black Soap or African Black Soap (Dudu Osun) while taking your spiritual bath.

## HOW TO DRESS A CANDLE FOR SPIRITUAL BATTLE

The magical power of the Quimbanda Spirits is more than just saying a few ritual words over a lit candle. The real magic is in your ability to raise the energy before and during any ritual. Experienced Quimbandeiros know that magical spells are never something to rush through. Every step of the magical ritual, from the moment you begin planning the spell, lends and gives energy to it. One important step in candle magic is dressing a candle, which helps to charge and consecrate the candle to match your intent. The following Quimbanda ritual candle formulas can be used when preparing for or during a spiritual battle.

### *RITUAL NOTES FOR A SUCCESSFUL CANDLE RITUAL*

When preparing and dressing a candle to banish away negative vibrations or to reverse and return a spell back to your enemies always dress the candle using your hands by starting to rub the prepared candle dressing oil from the middle of the candle, rub oil from middle to top for to "Banish" energy away from you. If you are preparing and dressing a candle to bring a good vibration back to your house after a spiritual attack then always the dress the candle using your hands by starting to rub the prepared candle dressing oil from middle to bottom to "Attract" energy to you. Remember both glass encased candles, pull out candles, image candles, pillar candles and taper candles are all ritually dressed and prepared in the same magical manner. The type of candle will depend on the individual's preference. I always prefer to use the old standard pillar or taper candles in my magical rituals. The choice is up to you. The only difference between using a glass encased candle for magical rituals as opposed to the other candles is that when you carve your intentions on the pull out candles, image candles, pillar candles and taper candles it is much easier. When using glass encased candles you can carve your intentions on the open flat wax top of candle and also use a permanent colored ink marker to write your intentions around the outside of the glass of the candle.

## THE GREAT QUIMBANDA RITUAL OF EXU TO DEFEAT YOUR ENEMIES

The following is a seven day ritual that is guaranteed to defeat any and all of your occult enemies. This includes both known and unknown enemies. The ritual ceremony must be done directly in front of the altar of the Quimbanda Trinity at 12 Midnight. If you have the actual Mysteries of the deity spirits of the Quimbanda Trinity, (The Nganga of Exu Maioral, the Nganga of Exu Rei and the Nganga of Maria Padilla Reina) you should send out their spirits using fula (gun powder) on the length of their sacred swords that each one has in their Ngangas. This should be done at the conclusion of each ritual when invoking and summoning their sacred powers and mysteries.

*ALWAYS TAKE A QUIMBANDA CLEANSING BATH AT THE CONCLUSION OF EACH RITUAL.*

## FRIDAY - 12 MIDNIGHT - THE FIRST DAY OF THE RITUAL

Burn Quimbanda Ritual Incense in the magical ritual area where you will be doing the ceremony.

Draw the Quimbanda spirit signature that represents the First Lesser Quimbanda Kingdom on the floor using red pemba (ritual chalk) directly in front of the altar of the Quimbanda Trinity deities.

Draw the Quimbanda spirit signature for Exu Rei Das Encruzilhadas on the floor using black pemba (ritual chalk) on the left side of the spirit signature that represents the First Lesser Quimbanda Kingdom.

Draw the Quimbanda spirit signature for Pomba Gira Reina Das Encruzilhadas on the floor using white pemba (ritual chalk) on the left side of the spirit signature that represents the First Lesser Quimbanda Kingdom.

Place a red candle on top of the spirit signature that represents the First Lesser Quimbanda Kingdom.

Place a black candle on top of the spirit signature that represents Exu Rei Das Encruzilhadas.

Place a red candle on top of the spirit signature that represents Pomba Gira Reina Das Encruzilhadas.

Begin the Quimbanda ritual by lighting the red candle first, the black candle second and the white candle last.

While lighting the candles recite the following ritual prayers:

*IN THE NAME OF NZAMBI, THE GOD OF THE HEAVENS AND THE EARTH - SARAVA*
*IN THE NAME OF EXU MAIORAL - SARAVA*
*IN THE NAME OF EXU REI - SARAVA*

*IN THE NAME OF MARIA PADILLA REINA – SARAVA*
*IN THE NAME OF THE QUIMBANDA TRINITY - SARAVA*
*I, say your complete birth name, INVOKE YOUR SACRED AND DIVINE POWERS IN THE NAME OF DIVINE JUSTICE.*

*BY THE DIVINE POWER OF KING* **EXU REI DAS ENCRUZILHADAS** *& QUEEN* **POMBA GIRA REINA DAS ENCRUZILHADAS** *OF THE KINGDOM OF THE CROSSROADS, I DO INVOKE AND DO SUMMON THE GUARDIAN SPIRITS WHICH PROTECT THIS REALM AND GIVE LIFE TO THIS SACRED RITUAL. BY THE DIVINE SWORD OF KING EXU REI DAS ENCRUZILHADAS & QUEEN POMBA GIRA REINA DAS ENCRUZILHADAS, I DO SUMMON AND I DO COMMAND THE GUARDIAN SPIRITS OF THE CROSSROADS IN THE NAME OF DIVINE JUSTICE TO DESTROY MY ENEMIES KNOWN AND UNKNOWN. I INVOKE THE POWERS OF THE QUIMBANDA CROSS TO COVER MY BODY IN PROTECTIVE LIGHT SO THAT MY ENEMIES KNOWN AND UNKNOW WILL NOT BE ABLE TO SEE NOR HEAR THIS SACRED RITUAL. I INVOKE AND SUMMON THE CHIEF SPIRIT, EXU TRANCA RUAS, TO BIND, BLIND, DESTROY AND CONQUER MY ENEMIES. O MOST GLORIOUS CHIEF SPIRIT,* **EXU TRANCA RUAS***, MY ENEMIES ARE YOUR ENEMIES AND YOUR ENEMIES ARE MY ENEMIES. O MOST GLORIOUS CHIEF SPIRIT, EXU TRANCA RUAS, GUARDIAN OF THE REINO DAS ENCRUZILHADAS, I LAY MY ENEMIES AT YOUR FEET. I INVOKE AND SUMMON THE CHIEF SPIRIT,* **EXU SETE ENCUZILHADAS***, TO BIND, BLIND, DESTROY AND CONQUER MY ENEMIES. O MOST GLORIOUS CHIEF SPIRIT, EXU SETE ENCUZILHADAS, MY ENEMIES ARE YOUR ENEMIES AND YOUR ENEMIES ARE MY ENEMIES. O MOST GLORIOUS CHIEF SPIRIT, EXU SETE ENCUZILHADAS, GUARDIAN OF THE REINO DAS ENCRUZILHADAS, I LAY MY ENEMIES AT YOUR FEET. I INVOKE AND SUMMON THE CHIEF SPIRIT,* **EXU DAS ALMAS***, TO BIND, BLIND, DESTROY AND CONQUER MY ENEMIES. O MOST GLORIOUS CHIEF SPIRIT, EXU DAS ALMAS, MY ENEMIES ARE YOUR ENEMIES AND YOUR ENEMIES ARE MY ENEMIES. O MOST GLORIOUS CHIEF SPIRIT, EXU DAS ALMAS, GUARDIAN OF THE REINO DAS ENCRUZILHADAS, I LAY MY ENEMIES AT YOUR FEET. I INVOKE AND SUMMON THE CHIEF SPIRIT,* **EXU MARABO***, TO*

*BIND, BLIND, DESTROY AND CONQUER MY ENEMIES. O MOST GLORIOUS CHIEF SPIRIT, EXU MARABO, MY ENEMIES ARE YOUR ENEMIES AND YOUR ENEMIES ARE MY ENEMIES. O MOST GLORIOUS CHIEF SPIRIT, EXU MARABO, GUARDIAN OF THE REINO DAS ENCRUZILHADAS, I LAY MY ENEMIES AT YOUR FEET. I INVOKE AND SUMMON THE CHIEF SPIRIT, EXU TIRIRI, TO BIND, BLIND, DESTROY AND CONQUER MY ENEMIES. O MOST GLORIOUS CHIEF SPIRIT,* ***EXU TIRIRI****, MY ENEMIES ARE YOUR ENEMIES AND YOUR ENEMIES ARE MY ENEMIES. O MOST GLORIOUS CHIEF SPIRIT, EXU TIRIRI, GUARDIAN OF THE REINO DAS ENCRUZILHADAS, I LAY MY ENEMIES AT YOUR FEET. I INVOKE AND SUMMON THE CHIEF SPIRIT,* **EXU VELUDO***, TO BIND, BLIND, DESTROY AND CONQUER MY ENEMIES. O MOST GLORIOUS CHIEF SPIRIT, EXU VELUDO, MY ENEMIES ARE YOUR ENEMIES AND YOUR ENEMIES ARE MY ENEMIES. O MOST GLORIOUS CHIEF SPIRIT, EXU VELUDO, GUARDIAN OF THE REINO DAS ENCRUZILHADAS, I LAY MY ENEMIES AT YOUR FEET. I INVOKE AND SUMMON THE CHIEF SPIRIT, EXU MORCEGO, TO BIND, BLIND, DESTROY AND CONQUER MY ENEMIES. O MOST GLORIOUS CHIEF SPIRIT,* **EXU MORCEGO***, MY ENEMIES ARE YOUR ENEMIES AND YOUR ENEMIES ARE MY ENEMIES. O MOST GLORIOUS CHIEF SPIRIT, EXU MORCEGO, GUARDIAN OF THE REINO DAS ENCRUZILHADAS, I LAY MY ENEMIES AT YOUR FEET. I INVOKE AND SUMMON THE CHIEF SPIRIT, EXU SETE GARGALHADAS, TO BIND, BLIND, DESTROY AND CONQUER MY ENEMIES. O MOST GLORIOUS CHIEF SPIRIT,* **EXU SETE GARGALHADAS***, MY ENEMIES ARE YOUR ENEMIES AND YOUR ENEMIES ARE MY ENEMIES. O MOST GLORIOUS CHIEF SPIRIT, EXU SETE GARGALHADAS, GUARDIAN OF THE REINO DAS ENCRUZILHADAS, I LAY MY ENEMIES AT YOUR FEET. I INVOKE AND SUMMON THE CHIEF SPIRIT,* **EXU MIRIM***, TO BIND, BLIND, DESTROY AND CONQUER MY ENEMIES. O MOST GLORIOUS CHIEF SPIRIT, EXU MIRIM, MY ENEMIES ARE YOUR ENEMIES AND YOUR ENEMIES ARE MY ENEMIES.O MOST GLORIOUS CHIEF SPIRIT, EXU MIRIM, GUARDIAN OF THE REINO DAS ENCRUZILHADAS, I LAY MY ENEMIES AT YOUR FEET. BY THE POWER AND THE VIRTUES OF THE GUARDIANS OF THE SACRED*

*SEVEN QUIMBANDA KINGDOMS,* ***EXU TRANCA RUAS, EXU SETE ENCRUZILHADAS, EXU DAS ALMAS, EXU MARABO, EXU TIRIRI, EXU VELUDO, EXU MORCEGO, EXU SETE GARGALHADAS,*** *AND* ***EXU MIRIM,*** *I DO SUMMON YOU HERE O POWERFUL QUIMBANDA SPIRITS AND COMMAND THIS RITUAL INTO BEING. IN THE NAME OF THE QUIMBANDA TRINITY AND LAWS OF DIVINE JUSTICE -* ***SARAVA***

*STATE YOUR REQUEST HERE & MEDITATE ON YOUR DESIRES*

## SATURDAY - 12 MIDNIGHT - THE SECOND DAY OF THE RITUAL

Burn Quimbanda Ritual Incense in the magical ritual area where you will be doing the ceremony.

Draw the Quimbanda spirit signature that represents the Second Lesser Quimbanda Kingdom on the floor using red pemba (ritual chalk) directly in front of the altar of the Quimbanda Trinity deities.

Draw the Quimbanda spirit signature for Exu Rei Dos 7 Cruzeiros on the floor using black pemba (ritual chalk) on the left side of the spirit signature that represents the Second Lesser Quimbanda Kingdom.

Draw the Quimbanda spirit signature for Pomba Gira Reina Dos 7 Cruzeiros on the floor using white pemba (ritual chalk) on the left side of the spirit signature that represents the Second Lesser Quimbanda Kingdom.

Place a red candle on top of the spirit signature that represents the Second Lesser Quimbanda Kingdom.

Place a black candle on top of the spirit signature that represents Exu Rei Dos 7 Cruzeiros.
Place a red candle on top of the spirit signature that represents Pomba Gira Reina Dos 7 Cruzeiros.

Begin the Quimbanda ritual by lighting the red candle first, the black candle second and the white candle last.

While lighting the candles recite the following ritual prayers:

*IN THE NAME OF NZAMBI, THE GOD OF THE HEAVENS AND THE EARTH - SARAVA*
*IN THE NAME OF EXU MAIORAL - SARAVA*
*IN THE NAME OF EXU REI - SARAVA*
*IN THE NAME OF MARIA PADILLA REINA – SARAVA*

*IN THE NAME OF THE QUIMBANDA TRINITY - SARAVA*

*I, say your complete birth name, INVOKE YOUR SACRED AND DIVINE POWERS IN THE NAME OF DIVINE JUSTICE. BY THE DIVINE POWER OF KING* ***EXU REI DOS 7 CRUZEIROS*** *& QUEEN* ***POMBA GIRA REINA DOS 7 CRUZEIROS*** *OF THE KINGDOM OF THE CROSINGSS, I DO INVOKE AND DO SUMMON THE GUARDIAN SPIRITS WHICH PROTECT THIS REALM AND GIVE LIFE TO THIS SACRED RITUAL. BY THE DIVINE SWORD OF KING EXU REI DOS 7 CRUZEIROS & QUEEN POMBA GIRA REINA DOS 7 CRUZEIROS, I DO SUMMON AND I DO COMMAND THE GUARDIAN SPIRITS OF THE CROSSINGS IN THE NAME OF DIVINE JUSTICE TO DESTROY MY ENEMIES KNOWN AND UNKNOWN. I INVOKE THE POWERS OF THE QUIMBANDA CROSS TO COVER MY BODY IN PROTECTIVE LIGHT SO THAT MY ENEMIES KNOWN AND UNKNOW WILL NOT BE ABLE TO SEE NOR HEAR THIS SACRED RITUAL. I INVOKE AND SUMMON THE CHIEF SPIRIT,* ***EXU TRANCA TUDO****, TO BIND, BLIND, DESTROY AND CONQUER MY ENEMIES.O MOST GLORIOUS CHIEF SPIRIT, EXU TRANCA TUDO, MY ENEMIES ARE YOUR ENEMIES AND YOUR ENEMIES ARE MY ENEMIES. O MOST GLORIOUS CHIEF SPIRIT, EXU TRANCA TUDO, GUARDIAN OF THE REINO DOS CRUZEIROS, I LAY MY ENEMIES AT YOUR FEET. I INVOKE AND SUMMON THE CHIEF SPIRIT,* ***EXU KIROMBO****, TO BIND, BLIND, DESTROY AND CONQUER MY ENEMIES. O MOST GLORIOUS CHIEF SPIRIT, EXU KIROMBO, MY ENEMIES ARE YOUR ENEMIES AND YOUR ENEMIES ARE MY ENEMIES. O MOST GLORIOUS CHIEF SPIRIT, EXU KIROMBO, GUARDIAN OF THE REINO DOS CRUZEIROS, I LAY MY ENEMIES AT YOUR FEET. I INVOKE AND SUMMON THE CHIEF SPIRIT,* ***EXU SETE CRUZEIROS****, TO BIND, BLIND, DESTROY AND CONQUER MY ENEMIES. O MOST GLORIOUS CHIEF SPIRIT, EXU SETE CRUZEIROS, MY ENEMIES ARE YOUR ENEMIES AND YOUR ENEMIES ARE MY ENEMIES. O MOST GLORIOUS CHIEF SPIRIT, EXU SETE CRUZEIROS, GUARDIAN OF THE REINO DOS CRUZEIROS, I LAY MY ENEMIES AT YOUR FEET. I INVOKE AND SUMMON THE CHIEF SPIRIT,* ***EXU MANGUEIRA****, TO BIND, BLIND, DESTROY AND CONQUER MY ENEMIES. O MOST GLORIOUS CHIEF SPIRIT, EXU MANGUEIRA, MY ENEMIES ARE YOUR ENEMIES AND YOUR ENEMIES ARE MY*

*ENEMIES. O MOST GLORIOUS CHIEF SPIRIT, EXU MANGUEIRA, GUARDIAN OF THE REINO DOS CRUZEIROS, I LAY MY ENEMIES AT YOUR FEET. I INVOKE AND SUMMON THE CHIEF SPIRIT,* ***EXU KAMINALOA****, TO BIND, BLIND, DESTROY AND CONQUER MY ENEMIES. O MOST GLORIOUS CHIEF SPIRIT, EXU KAMINALOA, MY ENEMIES ARE YOUR ENEMIES AND YOUR ENEMIES ARE MY ENEMIES. O MOST GLORIOUS CHIEF SPIRIT,* ***EXU KAMINALOA****, GUARDIAN OF THE REINO DOS CRUZEIROS, I LAY MY ENEMIES AT YOUR FEET. I INVOKE AND SUMMON THE CHIEF SPIRIT,* ***EXU SETE CRUZES****, TO BIND, BLIND, DESTROY AND CONQUER MY ENEMIES.O MOST GLORIOUS CHIEF SPIRIT, EXU SETE CRUZES, MY ENEMIES ARE YOUR ENEMIES AND YOUR ENEMIES ARE MY ENEMIES.O MOST GLORIOUS CHIEF SPIRIT, EXU SETE CRUZES, GUARDIAN OF THE REINO DOS CRUZEIROS, I LAY MY ENEMIES AT YOUR FEET. I INVOKE AND SUMMON THE CHIEF SPIRIT, EXU SETE PORTAS, TO BIND, BLIND, DESTROY AND CONQUER MY ENEMIES. O MOST GLORIOUS CHIEF SPIRIT,* ***EXU SETE PORTAS****, MY ENEMIES ARE YOUR ENEMIES AND YOUR ENEMIES ARE MY ENEMIES. O MOST GLORIOUS CHIEF SPIRIT, EXU SETE PORTAS, GUARDIAN OF THE REINO DOS CRUZEIROS, I LAY MY ENEMIES AT YOUR FEET. I INVOKE AND SUMMON THE CHIEF SPIRIT, EXU MEIA NOITE, TO BIND, BLIND, DESTROY AND CONQUER MY ENEMIES. O MOST GLORIOUS CHIEF SPIRIT,* ***EXU MEIA NOITE****, MY ENEMIES ARE YOUR ENEMIES AND YOUR ENEMIES ARE MY ENEMIES. O MOST GLORIOUS CHIEF SPIRIT, EXU MEIA NOITE, GUARDIAN OF THE REINO DOS CRUZEIROS, I LAY MY ENEMIES AT YOUR FEET. I INVOKE AND SUMMON THE CHIEF SPIRIT,* ***EXU KALUNGA****, TO BIND, BLIND, DESTROY AND CONQUER MY ENEMIES. O MOST GLORIOUS CHIEF SPIRIT, EXU CALUNGA, MY ENEMIES ARE YOUR ENEMIES AND YOUR ENEMIES ARE MY ENEMIES. O MOST GLORIOUS CHIEF SPIRIT, EXU KALUNGA, GUARDIAN OF THE REINO DOS CRUZEIROS, I LAY MY ENEMIES AT YOUR FEET. BY THE POWER AND THE VIRTUES OF THE DIVINE GUARDIANS OF THE SACRED SEVEN QUIMBANDA KINGDOMS,* ***EXU TRANCA TUDO****,* ***EXU KIROMBO****,* ***EXU SETE CRUZEIROS****,* ***EXU MANGUEIRA****,* ***EXU KAMINALOA****,* ***EXU*** *SETE CRUZES,* ***EXU MEIA NOITE*** *AND* ***EXU KALUNGA****, I DO SUMMON YOU HERE O POWERFUL QUIMBANDA SPIRITS AND COMMAND THIS RITUAL*

*INTO BEING. IN THE NAME OF THE QUIMBANDA TRINITY AND LAWS OF DIVINE JUSTICE -* ***SARAVA***

*STATE YOUR REQUEST HERE & MEDITATE ON YOUR DESIRES*

**SUNDAY - 12 MIDNIGHT - THE THIRD DAY OF THE RITUAL**

Burn Quimbanda Ritual Incense in the magical ritual area where you will be doing the ceremony.

Draw the Quimbanda spirit signature that represents the Third Lesser Quimbanda Kingdom on the floor using red pemba (ritual chalk) directly in front of the altar of the Quimbanda Trinity deities.

Draw the Quimbanda spirit signature for Exu Rei Das Matas on the floor using black pemba (ritual chalk) on the left side of the spirit signature that represents the Third Lesser Quimbanda Kingdom.

Draw the Quimbanda spirit signature for Pomba Gira Reina Das Matas on the floor using white pemba (ritual chalk) on the left side of the spirit signature that represents the Third Lesser Quimbanda Kingdom.

Place a red candle on top of the spirit signature that represents the Third Lesser Quimbanda Kingdom.

Place a black candle on top of the spirit signature that represents Exu Rei Das Matas.

Place a red candle on top of the spirit signature that represents Pomba Gira Reina Das Matas.

Begin the Quimbanda ritual by lighting the red candle first, the black candle second and the white candle last.

While lighting the candles recite the following ritual prayers:

*IN THE NAME OF NZAMBI, THE GOD OF THE HEAVENS AND THE EARTH - SARAVA*
*IN THE NAME OF EXU MAIORAL - SARAVA*
*IN THE NAME OF EXU REI - SARAVA*

*IN THE NAME OF MARIA PADILLA REINA – SARAVA*
*IN THE NAME OF THE QUIMBANDA TRINITY - SARAVA*
*I, say your complete birth name, INVOKE YOUR SACRED AND DIVINE POWERS IN THE NAME OF DIVINE JUSTICE. BY THE DIVINE POWER OF KING* **EXU REI DAS MATAS** *& QUEEN* **POMBA GIRA REINA DAS MATAS** *OF THE KINGDOM OF THE FORESTS, I DO INVOKE AND DO SUMMON THE GUARDIAN SPIRITS WHICH PROTECT THIS REALM AND GIVE LIFE TO THIS SACRED RITUAL. BY THE DIVINE SWORD OF KING EXU REI DAS MATAS & QUEEN POMBA GIRA REINA DAS MATAS, I DO SUMMON AND I DO COMMAND THE GUARDIAN SPIRITS OF THE FORESTS IN THE NAME OF DIVINE JUSTICE TO DESTROY MY ENEMIES KNOWN AND UNKNOWN.I INVOKE THE POWERS OF THE QUIMBANDA CROSS TO COVER MY BODY IN PROTECTIVE LIGHT SO THAT MY ENEMIES KNOWN AND UNKNOW WILL NOT BE ABLE TO SEE NOR HEAR THIS SACRED RITUAL. I INVOKE AND SUMMON THE CHIEF SPIRIT,* **EXU QUEBRA GALHO***, TO BIND, BLIND, DESTROY AND CONQUER MY ENEMIES. O MOST GLORIOUS EXU SPIRIT, EXU QUEBRA GALHO, MY ENEMIES ARE YOUR ENEMIES AND YOUR ENEMIES ARE MY ENEMIES. O MOST GLORIOUS EXU SPIRIT, EXU QUEBRA GALHO, GUARDIAN OF THE REINO DAS MATAS, I LAY MY ENEMIES AT YOUR FEET. I INVOKE AND SUMMON THE CHIEF SPIRIT,* **EXU DAS SOMBRAS***, TO BIND, BLIND, DESTROY AND CONQUER MY ENEMIES. O MOST GLORIOUS CHIEF SPIRIT, EXU DAS SOMBRAS, MY ENEMIES ARE YOUR ENEMIES AND YOUR ENEMIES ARE MY ENEMIES. O MOST GLORIOUS CHIEF SPIRIT, EXU DAS SOMBRAS, GUARDIAN OF THE REINO DAS MATAS, I LAY MY ENEMIES AT YOUR FEET. I INVOKE AND SUMMON THE CHIEF SPIRIT, EXU DAS MATAS, TO BIND, BLIND, DESTROY AND CONQUER MY ENEMIES. O MOST GLORIOUS CHIEF SPIRIT,* **EXU DAS MATAS***, MY ENEMIES ARE YOUR ENEMIES AND YOUR ENEMIES ARE MY ENEMIES. O MOST GLORIOUS CHIEF SPIRIT, EXU DAS MATAS, GUARDIAN OF THE REINO DAS MATAS, I LAY MY ENEMIES AT YOUR FEET. I INVOKE AND SUMMON THE CHIEF SPIRIT, EXU DAS CAMPINAS, TO BIND, BLIND, DESTROY AND CONQUER MY ENEMIES. O MOST GLORIOUS CHIEF SPIRIT,* **EXU DAS CAMPINAS***, MY ENEMIES ARE YOUR ENEMIES*

*AND YOUR ENEMIES ARE MY ENEMIES. O MOST GLORIOUS CHIEF SPIRIT, EXU DAS CAMPINAS, GUARDIAN OF THE REINO DAS MATAS, I LAY MY ENEMIES AT YOUR FEET. I INVOKE AND SUMMON THE CHIEF SPIRIT,* **EXU DA SERRA NEGRA***, TO BIND, BLIND, DESTROY AND CONQUER MY ENEMIES. O MOST GLORIOUS CHIEF SPIRIT, EXU DA SERRA NEGRA, MY ENEMIES ARE YOUR ENEMIES AND YOUR ENEMIES ARE MY ENEMIES. O MOST GLORIOUS CHIEF SPIRIT, EXU DA SERRA NEGRA, GUARDIAN OF THE REINO DAS MATAS, I LAY MY ENEMIES AT YOUR FEET. I INVOKE AND SUMMON THE SPIRIT* **EXU SETE PEDRAS***, TO BIND, BLIND, DESTROY AND CONQUER MY ENEMIES. O MOST GLORIOUS SPIRIT EXU SETE PEDRAS, MY ENEMIES ARE YOUR ENEMIES AND YOUR ENEMIES ARE MY ENEMIES. O MOST GLORIOUS SPIRIT EXU SETE PEDRAS, GUARDIAN OF THE REINO DAS MATAS, I LAY MY ENEMIES AT YOUR FEET. I INVOKE AND SUMMON THE CHIEF SPIRIT, EXU SETE COBRAS, TO BIND, BLIND, DESTROY AND CONQUER MY ENEMIES. O MOST GLORIOUS CHIEF SPIRIT, EXU* **SETE COBRAS***, MY ENEMIES ARE YOUR ENEMIES AND YOUR ENEMIES ARE MY ENEMIES. O MOST GLORIOUS CHIEF SPIRIT, EXU SETE COBRAS, GUARDIAN OF THE REINO DAS MATAS, I LAY MY ENEMIES AT YOUR FEET. I INVOKE AND SUMMON THE CHIEF SPIRIT,* **EXU DO CHEIRO***, TO BIND, BLIND, DESTROY AND CONQUER MY ENEMIES. O MOST GLORIOUS CHIEF SPIRIT, EXU DO CHEIRO, MY ENEMIES ARE YOUR ENEMIES AND YOUR ENEMIES ARE MY ENEMIES. O MOST GLORIOUS CHIEF SPIRIT, EXU DO CHEIRO, GUARDIAN OF THE REINO DAS MATAS, I LAY MY ENEMIES AT YOUR FEET. I INVOKE AND SUMMON THE CHIEF SPIRIT, EXU ARRANCA TOCO, TO BIND, BLIND, DESTROY AND CONQUER MY ENEMIES. O MOST GLORIOUS CHIEF SPIRIT,* **EXU ARRANCA TOCO***, MY ENEMIES ARE YOUR ENEMIES AND YOUR ENEMIES ARE MY ENEMIES. O MOST GLORIOUS CHIEF SPIRIT, EXU ARRANCA TOCO, GUARDIAN OF THE REINO DAS MATAS, I LAY MY ENEMIES AT YOUR FEET. BY THE POWER AND THE VIRTUES OF THE DIVINE GUARDIANS OF THE SACRED SEVEN QUIMBANDA KINGDOMS,* **EXU QUEBRA GALHO***,* **EXU DAS SOMBRAS***,* **EXU DAS MATAS***,* **EXU DAS CAMPINAS***,* **EXU DA SERRA NEGRA***,* **EXU SETE PEDRAS***,* **EXU SETE COBRAS***,* **EXU DO**

***CHEIRO*** *AND* ***EXU ARRANCA TOCO****, I DO SUMMON YOU HERE O POWERFUL QUIMBANDA SPIRITS AND COMMAND THIS RITUAL INTO BEING. IN THE NAME OF THE QUIMBANDA TRINITY AND LAWS OF DIVINE JUSTICE -* ***SARAVA***

*STATE YOUR REQUEST HERE & MEDITATE ON YOUR DESIRES*

## MONDAY - 12 MIDNIGHT - THE FOURTH DAY OF THE RITUAL

Burn Quimbanda Ritual Incense in the magical ritual area where you will be doing the ceremony.

Draw the Quimbanda spirit signature that represents the Fourth Lesser Quimbanda Kingdom on the floor using red pemba (ritual chalk) directly in front of the altar of the Quimbanda Trinity deities.

Draw the Quimbanda spirit signature for Exu Rei Da Kalunga on the floor using black pemba (ritual chalk) on the left side of the spirit signature that represents the Fourth Lesser Quimbanda Kingdom.

Draw the Quimbanda spirit signature for Pomba Gira Reina Da Kalunga on the floor using white pemba (ritual chalk) on the left side of the spirit signature that represents the Fourth Lesser Quimbanda Kingdom.

Place a red candle on top of the spirit signature that represents the Fourth Lesser Quimbanda Kingdom. Place a black candle on top of the spirit signature that represents Exu Rei Da Kalunga. Place a red candle on top of the spirit signature that represents Pomba Gira Reina Da Kalunga. Begin the Quimbanda ritual by lighting the red candle first, the black candle second and the white candle last.

While lighting the candles recite the following ritual prayers:

*IN THE NAME OF NZAMBI, THE GOD OF THE HEAVENS AND THE EARTH - SARAVA*
*IN THE NAME OF EXU MAIORAL - SARAVA*
*IN THE NAME OF EXU REI - SARAVA*
*IN THE NAME OF MARIA PADILLA REINA – SARAVA*
*IN THE NAME OF THE QUIMBANDA TRINITY - SARAVA*
*I, say your complete birth name, INVOKE YOUR SACRED AND DIVINE POWERS IN THE NAME OF DIVINE JUSTICE. BY THE*

*DIVINE POWER OF KING* **EXU REI DA KALUNGA** *& QUEEN* **POMBA GIRA REINA DA KALUNGA** *OF THE KINGDOM OF THE CEMETERY, I DO INVOKE AND DO SUMMON THE GUARDIAN SPIRITS WHICH PROTECT THIS REALM AND GIVE LIFE TO THIS SACRED RITUAL. BY THE DIVINE SWORD OF KING EXU REI DA KALUNGA & QUEEN POMBA GIRA REINA DA KALUNGA, I DO SUMMON AND I DO COMMAND THE GUARDIAN SPIRITS OF THE CEMETERY IN THE NAME OF DIVINE JUSTICE TO DESTROY MY ENEMIES KNOWN AND UNKNOWN. I INVOKE THE POWERS OF THE QUIMBANDA CROSS TO COVER MY BODY IN PROTECTIVE LIGHT SO THAT MY ENEMIES KNOWN AND UNKNOW WILL NOT BE ABLE TO SEE NOR HEAR THIS SACRED RITUAL. I INVOKE AND SUMMON THE SPIRIT* **EXU PORTEIRA**, *TO BIND, BLIND, DESTROY AND CONQUER MY ENEMIES. O MOST GLORIOUS SPIRIT EXU PORTEIRA, MY ENEMIES ARE YOUR ENEMIES AND YOUR ENEMIES ARE MY ENEMIES. O MOST GLORIOUS SPIRIT EXU PORTEIRA, GUARDIAN OF THE REINO DA KALUNGA, I LAY MY ENEMIES AT YOUR FEET. I INVOKE AND SUMMON THE SPIRIT EXU SETE TUMBAS, TO BIND, BLIND, DESTROY AND CONQUER MY ENEMIES. O MOST GLORIOUS SPIRIT* **EXU SETE TUMBAS**, *MY ENEMIES ARE YOUR ENEMIES AND YOUR ENEMIES ARE MY ENEMIES. O MOST GLORIOUS SPIRIT EXU SETE TUMBAS, GUARDIAN OF THE REINO DA KALUNGA, I LAY MY ENEMIES AT YOUR FEET. I INVOKE AND SUMMON THE SPIRIT* **EXU SETE CATACUMBAS**, *TO BIND, BLIND, DESTROY AND CONQUER MY ENEMIES. O MOST GLORIOUS SPIRIT EXU SETE CATACUMBAS, MY ENEMIES ARE YOUR ENEMIES AND YOUR ENEMIES ARE MY ENEMIES. O MOST GLORIOUS SPIRIT EXU SETE CATACUMBAS, GUARDIAN OF THE REINO DA KALUNGA, I LAY MY ENEMIES AT YOUR FEET. I INVOKE AND SUMMON THE SPIRIT* **EXU DA BRASA**, *TO BIND, BLIND, DESTROY AND CONQUER MY ENEMIES. O MOST GLORIOUS SPIRIT EXU DA BRASA, MY ENEMIES ARE YOUR ENEMIES AND YOUR ENEMIES ARE MY ENEMIES. O MOST GLORIOUS SPIRIT EXU DA BRASA, GUARDIAN OF THE REINO DA KALUNGA, I LAY MY ENEMIES AT YOUR FEET. I INVOKE AND SUMMON THE SPIRIT* **EXU CAVEIRA**, *TO BIND, BLIND, DESTROY AND CONQUER MY ENEMIES. O MOST GLORIOUS SPIRIT EXU CAVEIRA, MY ENEMIES ARE YOUR*

*ENEMIES AND YOUR ENEMIES ARE MY ENEMIES. O MOST GLORIOUS SPIRIT EXU CAVEIRA, GUARDIAN OF THE REINO DA KALUNGA, I LAY MY ENEMIES AT YOUR FEET. I INVOKE AND SUMMON THE SPIRIT* **EXU KALUNGA PEQUENA**, *TO BIND, BLIND, DESTROY AND CONQUER MY ENEMIES. O MOST GLORIOUS SPIRIT* **KALUNGA PEQUENA**, *MY ENEMIES ARE YOUR ENEMIES AND YOUR ENEMIES ARE MY ENEMIES.O MOST GLORIOUS SPIRIT* **KALUNGA PEQUENA** *, GUARDIAN OF THE REINO DA KALUNGA, I LAY MY ENEMIES AT YOUR FEET. I INVOKE AND SUMMON THE SPIRIT* **EXU CORCUNDA**, *TO BIND, BLIND, DESTROY AND CONQUER MY ENEMIES. O MOST GLORIOUS SPIRIT EXU CORCUNDA, MY ENEMIES ARE YOUR ENEMIES AND YOUR ENEMIES ARE MY ENEMIES. O MOST GLORIOUS SPIRIT EXU CORCUNDA, GUARDIAN OF THE REINO DA KALUNGA, I LAY MY ENEMIES AT YOUR FEET. I INVOKE AND SUMMON THE SPIRIT* **EXU SETE COVAS**, *T O BIND, BLIND, DESTROY AND CONQUER MY ENEMIES. O MOST GLORIOUS SPIRIT EXU SETE COVAS, MY ENEMIES ARE YOUR ENEMIES AND YOUR ENEMIES ARE MY ENEMIES. O MOST GLORIOUS SPIRIT EXU SETE COVAS, GUARDIAN OF THE REINO DA KALUNGA, I LAY MY ENEMIES AT YOUR FEET. I INVOKE AND SUMMON THE SPIRIT* **EXU CAPA PRETA**, *TO BIND, BLIND, DESTROY AND CONQUER MY ENEMIES. O MOST GLORIOUS SPIRIT, EXU CAPA PRETA, MY ENEMIES ARE YOUR ENEMIES AND YOUR ENEMIES ARE MY ENEMIES. O MOST GLORIOUS SPIRIT EXU CAPA PRETA, GUARDIAN OF THE REINO DA KALUNGA, I LAY MY ENEMIES AT YOUR FEET. BY THE POWER AND THE VIRTUES OF THE DIVINE GUARDIANS OF THE SACRED SEVEN KINGDOMS,* **EXU PORTEIRA**, **EXU SETE TUMBAS**, **EXU SETE CATACUMBAS**, **EXU DA BRASA**, **EXU CAVEIRA**, **EXU KALUNGA**, **EXU CORCUNDA**, **EXU SETE COVAS** *AND* **EXU CAPA PRETA**, *I DO SUMMON YOU HERE O POWERFUL QUIMBANDA SPIRITS AND COMMAND THIS RITUAL INTO BEING. IN THE NAME OF THE QUIMBANDA TRINITY AND LAWS OF DIVINE JUSTICE -* **SARAVA**

*STATE YOUR REQUEST HERE & MEDITATE ON YOUR DESIRES*

## TUESDAY - 12 MIDNIGHT - THE FIFTH DAY OF THE RITUAL

Burn Quimbanda Ritual Incense in the magical ritual area where you will be doing the ceremony.

Draw the Quimbanda spirit signature that represents the Fifth Lesser Quimbanda Kingdom on the floor using red pemba (ritual chalk) directly in front of the altar of the Quimbanda Trinity deities.

Draw the Quimbanda spirit signature for Exu Rei Das Almas on the floor using black pemba (ritual chalk) on the left side of the spirit signature that represents the Fifth Lesser Quimbanda Kingdom.

Draw the Quimbanda spirit signature for Pomba Gira Reina Das Almas on the floor using white pemba (ritual chalk) on the left side of the spirit signature that represents the Fifth Lesser Quimbanda Kingdom.

Place a red candle on top of the spirit signature that represents the Fifth Lesser Quimbanda Kingdom.

Place a black candle on top of the spirit signature that represents Exu Rei Das Almas.

Place a red candle on top of the spirit signature that represents Pomba Gira Reina Das Almas.

Begin the Quimbanda ritual by lighting the red candle first, the black candle second and the white candle last.

While lighting the candles recite the following ritual prayers:

*IN THE NAME OF NZAMBI, THE GOD OF THE HEAVENS AND THE EARTH - SARAVA*
*IN THE NAME OF EXU MAIORAL - SARAVA*
*IN THE NAME OF EXU REI - SARAVA*

*IN THE NAME OF MARIA PADILLA REINA - SARAVA*
*IN THE NAME OF THE QUIMBANDA TRINITY - SARAVA*
*I, say your complete birth name, INVOKE YOUR SACRED AND DIVINE POWERS IN THE NAME OF DIVINE JUSTICE.*
*BY THE DIVINE POWER OF KING* ***EXU REI DAS ALMAS*** *& QUEEN* ***POMBA GIRA REINA DAS ALMAS*** *OF THE KINGDOM OF THE SOULS, I DO INVOKE AND DO SUMMON THE GUARDIAN SPIRITS WHICH PROTECT THIS REALM AND GIVE LIFE TO THIS SACRED RITUAL. BY THE DIVINE SWORD OF KING EXU REI DAS ALMAS & QUEEN POMBA GIRA REINA DAS ALMAS, I DO SUMMON AND I DO COMMAND THE GUARDIAN SPIRITS OF THE REALM OF THE SOULS IN THE NAME OF DIVINE JUSTICE TO DESTROY MY ENEMIES KNOWN AND UNKNOWN. I INVOKE THE POWERS OF THE QUIMBANDA CROSS TO COVER MY BODY IN PROTECTIVE LIGHT SO THAT MY ENEMIES KNOWN AND UNKNOW WILL NOT BE ABLE TO SEE NOR HEAR THIS SACRED RITUAL. I INVOKE AND SUMMON THE CHIEF SPIRIT,* ***EXU SETE LOMBAS****, TO BIND, BLIND, DESTROY AND CONQUER MY ENEMIES. O MOST GLORIOUS CHIEF SPIRIT, EXU SETE LOMBAS, MY ENEMIES ARE YOUR ENEMIES AND YOUR ENEMIES ARE MY ENEMIES. O MOST GLORIOUS CHIEF SPIRIT, EXU SETE LOMBAS, GUARDIAN OF THE REINO DAS ALMAS, I LAY MY ENEMIES AT YOUR FEET. I INVOKE AND SUMMON THE CHIEF SPIRIT,* ***EXU PEMBA****, TO BIND, BLIND, DESTROY AND CONQUER MY ENEMIES. O MOST GLORIOUS CHIEF SPIRIT, EXU PEMBA, MY ENEMIES ARE YOUR ENEMIES AND YOUR ENEMIES ARE MY ENEMIES. O MOST GLORIOUS CHIEF SPIRIT, EXU PEMBA, GUARDIAN OF THE REINO DAS ALMAS, I LAY MY ENEMIES AT YOUR FEET. I INVOKE AND SUMMON THE CHIEF SPIRIT,* ***EXU MARABA****, TO BIND, BLIND, DESTROY AND CONQUER MY ENEMIES. O MOST GLORIOUS CHIEF SPIRIT, EXU MARABA, MY ENEMIES ARE YOUR ENEMIES AND YOUR ENEMIES ARE MY ENEMIES. O MOST GLORIOUS CHIEF SPIRIT, EXU MARABA, GUARDIAN OF THE REINO DAS ALMAS, I LAY MY ENEMIES AT YOUR FEET. I INVOKE AND SUMMON THE CHIEF SPIRIT, EXU CURADO, TO BIND, BLIND, DESTROY AND CONQUER MY ENEMIES.O MOST GLORIOUS CHIEF SPIRIT,* ***EXU CURADO****, MY ENEMIES ARE YOUR ENEMIES AND YOUR ENEMIES ARE MY*

*ENEMIES. O MOST GLORIOUS CHIEF SPIRIT, EXU CURADO, GUARDIAN OF THE REINO DAS ALMAS, I LAY MY ENEMIES AT YOUR FEET. I INVOKE AND SUMMON THE CHIEF SPIRIT,* **EXU NOVE LUZES**, *TO BIND, BLIND, DESTROY AND CONQUER MY ENEMIES. O MOST GLORIOUS CHIEF SPIRIT, EXU NOVE LUZES, MY ENEMIES ARE YOUR ENEMIES AND YOUR ENEMIES ARE MY ENEMIES. O MOST GLORIOUS CHIEF SPIRIT, EXU NOVE LUZES, GUARDIAN OF THE REINO DAS ALMAS, I LAY MY ENEMIES AT YOUR FEET. I INVOKE AND SUMMON THE CHIEF SPIRIT,* **EXU 7 MONTANHAS**, *TO BIND, BLIND, DESTROY AND CONQUER MY ENEMIES. O MOST GLORIOUS CHIEF SPIRIT, EXU 7 MONTANHAS, MY ENEMIES ARE YOUR ENEMIES AND YOUR ENEMIES ARE MY ENEMIES. O MOST GLORIOUS CHIEF SPIRIT, EXU 7 MONTANHAS, GUARDIAN OF THE REINO DAS ALMAS, I LAY MY ENEMIES AT YOUR FEET. I INVOKE AND SUMMON THE CHIEF SPIRIT,* **EXU TATA CAVEIRA**, *TO BIND, BLIND, DESTROY AND CONQUER MY ENEMIES. O MOST GLORIOUS CHIEF SPIRIT, EXU TATA CAVEIRA, MY ENEMIES ARE YOUR ENEMIES AND YOUR ENEMIES ARE MY ENEMIES.O MOST GLORIOUS CHIEF SPIRIT, EXU TATA CAVEIRA, GUARDIAN OF THE REINO DAS ALMAS, I LAY MY ENEMIES AT YOUR FEET. I INVOKE AND SUMMON THE CHIEF SPIRIT,* **EXU GIRA MUNDO**, *TO BIND, BLIND, DESTROY AND CONQUER MY ENEMIES. O MOST GLORIOUS CHIEF SPIRIT, EXU GIRA MUNDO, MY ENEMIES ARE YOUR ENEMIES AND YOUR ENEMIES ARE MY ENEMIES. O MOST GLORIOUS CHIEF SPIRIT, EXU GIRA MUNDO, GUARDIAN OF THE REINO DAS ALMAS, I LAY MY ENEMIES AT YOUR FEET. I INVOKE AND SUMMON THE CHIEF SPIRIT,* **EXU 7 POEIRAS**, *TO BIND, BLIND, DESTROY AND CONQUER MY ENEMIES. O MOST GLORIOUS CHIEF SPIRIT, EXU 7 POEIRAS, MY ENEMIES ARE YOUR ENEMIES AND YOUR ENEMIES ARE MY ENEMIES. O MOST GLORIOUS CHIEF SPIRIT, EXU 7 POEIRAS, GUARDIAN OF THE REINO DAS ALMAS, I LAY MY ENEMIES AT YOUR FEET. BY THE POWER AND THE VIRTUES OF THE GUARDIANS OF THE SACRED SEVEN QUIMBANDA KINGDOMS,* **EXU SETE LOMBAS**, **EXU PEMBA**, **EXU MARABA**, **EXU CURADO**, **EXU NOVE LUZES**, **EXU 7 MONTANHAS**, **EXU TATA CAVEIRA**, **EXU GIRA MUNDO** *AND* **EXU 7 POEIRAS**, *I DO SUMMON YOU HERE O POWERFUL*

*QUIMBANDA SPIRITS AND COMMAND THIS RITUAL INTO BEING. IN THE NAME OF THE QUIMBANDA TRINITY AND LAWS OF DIVINE JUSTICE -* **SARAVA**

*STATE YOUR REQUEST HERE & MEDITATE ON YOUR DESIRES*

**WEDNESDAY - 12 MIDNIGHT - THE SIXTH DAY OF THE RITUAL**

Burn Quimbanda Ritual Incense in the magical ritual area where you will be doing the ceremony.

Draw the Quimbanda spirit signature that represents the Sixth Lesser Quimbanda Kingdom on the floor using red pemba (ritual chalk) directly in front of the altar of the Quimbanda Trinity deities.

Draw the Quimbanda spirit signature for Exu Rei Das Liras on the floor using black pemba (ritual chalk) on the left side of the spirit signature that represents the Sixth Lesser Quimbanda Kingdom.

Draw the Quimbanda spirit signature for Pomba Gira Reina Das Liras on the floor using white pemba (ritual chalk) on the left side of the spirit signature that represents the Sixth Lesser Quimbanda Kingdom.

Place a red candle on top of the spirit signature that represents the Sixth Lesser Quimbanda Kingdom.

Place a black candle on top of the spirit signature that represents Exu Rei Das Liras. Place a red candle on top of the spirit signature that represents Pomba Gira Reina Das Liras.

Begin the Quimbanda ritual by lighting the red candle first, the black candle second and the white candle last.

While lighting the candles recite the following ritual prayers:

*IN THE NAME OF NZAMBI, THE GOD OF THE HEAVENS AND THE EARTH - SARAVA*
*IN THE NAME OF EXU MAIORAL - SARAVA*
*IN THE NAME OF EXU REI - SARAVA*
*IN THE NAME OF MARIA PADILLA REINA - SARAVA*
*IN THE NAME OF THE QUIMBANDA TRINITY - SARAVA*
*I, say your complete birth name, INVOKE YOUR SACRED AND DIVINE POWERS IN THE NAME OF DIVINE JUSTICE.*
*BY THE DIVINE POWER OF KING* ***EXU REI DAS LIRAS*** *& QUEEN* ***POMBA GIRA REINA DAS LIRAS*** *OF THE KINGDOM OF THE LYRE, I DO INVOKE AND DO SUMMON THE GUARDIAN SPIRITS WHICH PROTECT THIS REALM AND GIVE LIFE TO THIS SACRED RITUAL BY THE DIVINE SWORD OF KING EXU REI DAS LIRAS & QUEEN POMBA GIRA REINA DAS LIRAS, I DO SUMMON AND I DO COMMAND THE GUARDIAN SPIRITS OF THE REALM OF THE LYRE. IN THE NAME OF DIVINE JUSTICE TO DESTROY MY ENEMIES KNOWN AND UNKNOWN. I INVOKE THE POWERS OF THE QUIMBANDA CROSS TO COVER MY BODY IN PROTECTIVE LIGHT SO THAT MY ENEMIES KNOWN AND UNKNOW WILL NOT BE ABLE TO SEE NOR HEAR THIS SACRED RITUAL. I INVOKE AND SUMMON THE CHIEF SPIRIT,* ***EXU DOS INFERNOS****, TO BIND, BLIND, DESTROY AND CONQUER MY ENEMIES. O MOST GLORIOUS CHIEF SPIRIT, EXU DOS INFERNOS, MY ENEMIES ARE YOUR ENEMIES AND YOUR ENEMIES ARE MY ENEMIES. O MOST GLORIOUS CHIEF SPIRIT, EXU DOS INFERNOS, GUARDIAN OF THE REINO DA LIRA, I LAY MY ENEMIES AT YOUR FEET. I INVOKE AND SUMMON THE CHIEF SPIRIT,* ***EXU DOS CABARES****, TO BIND, BLIND, DESTROY AND CONQUER MY ENEMIES. O MOST GLORIOUS CHIEF SPIRIT, EXU DOS CABARES, MY ENEMIES ARE YOUR ENEMIES AND YOUR ENEMIES ARE MY ENEMIES. O MOST GLORIOUS CHIEF SPIRIT, EXU DOS CABARES, GUARDIAN OF THE REINO DA LIRA, I LAY MY ENEMIES AT YOUR FEET. I INVOKE AND SUMMON THE CHIEF SPIRIT,* ***EXU SETE LIRAS****, TO BIND,*

*BLIND, DESTROY AND CONQUER MY ENEMIES. O MOST GLORIOUS CHIEF SPIRIT, EXU SETE LIRAS, MY ENEMIES ARE YOUR ENEMIES AND YOUR ENEMIES ARE MY ENEMIES. O MOST GLORIOUS CHIEF SPIRIT, EXU SETE LIRAS, GUARDIAN OF THE REINO DA LIRA, I LAY MY ENEMIES AT YOUR FEET. I INVOKE AND SUMMON THE CHIEF SPIRIT,* **EXU CIGANO**, *TO BIND, BLIND, DESTROY AND CONQUER MY ENEMIES. O MOST GLORIOUS CHIEF SPIRIT, EXU CIGANO, MY ENEMIES ARE YOUR ENEMIES AND YOUR ENEMIES ARE MY ENEMIES. O MOST GLORIOUS CHIEF SPIRIT, EXU CIGANO, GUARDIAN OF THE REINO DA LIRA, I LAY MY ENEMIES AT YOUR FEET. I INVOKE AND SUMMON THE CHIEF SPIRIT,* **EXU ZE PELINTRA**, *TO BIND, BLIND, DESTROY AND CONQUER MY ENEMIES. O MOST GLORIOUS CHIEF SPIRIT, EXU ZE PELINTRA, MY ENEMIES ARE YOUR ENEMIES AND YOUR ENEMIES ARE MY ENEMIES. O MOST GLORIOUS CHIEF SPIRIT, EXU ZE PELINTRA, GUARDIAN OF THE REINO DA LIRA, I LAY MY ENEMIES AT YOUR FEET. I INVOKE AND SUMMON THE CHIEF SPIRIT,* **EXU PAGAO**, *TO BIND, BLIND, DESTROY AND CONQUER MY ENEMIES. O MOST GLORIOUS CHIEF SPIRIT, EXU PAGAO, MY ENEMIES ARE YOUR ENEMIES AND YOUR ENEMIES ARE MY ENEMIES. O MOST GLORIOUS CHIEF SPIRIT, EXU PAGAO, GUARDIAN OF THE REINO DA LIRA, I LAY MY ENEMIES AT YOUR FEET. I INVOKE AND SUMMON THE CHIEF SPIRIT,* **EXU DA GANGA**, *TO BIND, BLIND, DESTROY AND CONQUER MY ENEMIES. O MOST GLORIOUS CHIEF SPIRIT, EXU DA GANGA, MY ENEMIES ARE YOUR ENEMIES AND YOUR ENEMIES ARE MY ENEMIES. O MOST GLORIOUS CHIEF SPIRIT, EXU DA GANGA, GUARDIAN OF THE REINO DA LIRA, I LAY MY ENEMIES AT YOUR FEET. I INVOKE AND SUMMON THE CHIEF,* **EXU MALE**, *TO BIND, BLIND, DESTROY AND CONQUER MY ENEMIES. O MOST GLORIOUS CHIEF SPIRIT, EXU MALE, MY ENEMIES ARE YOUR ENEMIES AND YOUR ENEMIES ARE MY ENEMIES. O MOST GLORIOUS CHIEF SPIRIT, EXU MALE, GUARDIAN OF THE REINO DA LIRA, I LAY MY ENEMIES AT YOUR FEET. I INVOKE AND SUMMON THE CHIEF SPIRIT,* **EXU CHAMA DINHEIRO**, *TO BIND, BLIND, DESTROY AND CONQUER MY ENEMIES. O MOST GLORIOUS CHIEF SPIRIT, EXU CHAMA DINHEIRO, MY ENEMIES ARE YOUR ENEMIES AND YOUR*

*ENEMIES ARE MY ENEMIES. O MOST GLORIOUS CHIEF SPIRIT, EXU CHAMA DINHEIRO, GUARDIAN OF THE REINO DA LIRA, I LAY MY ENEMIES AT YOUR FEET. BY THE POWER AND THE VIRTUES OF THE GUARDIANS OF THE SACRED SEVEN QUIMBANDA KINGDOMS,* ***EXU DOS INFERNOS****,* ***EXU DOS CABARES****,* ***EXU SETE LIRAS****,* ***EXU CIGANO****,* ***EXU ZE PELINTRA****,* ***EXU PAGAO****,* ***EXU DA GANGA****,* ***EXU MALE*** *AND* ***EXU CHAMA DINHEIRO****, I DO SUMMON YOU HERE O POWERFUL QUIMBANDA SPIRITS AND COMMAND THIS RITUAL INTO BEING. IN THE NAME OF THE QUIMBANDA TRINITY AND LAWS OF DIVINE JUSTICE -* ***SARAVA***

*STATE YOUR REQUEST HERE & MEDITATE ON YOUR DESIRES*

## THURSDAY - 12 MIDNIGHT - THE SEVENTH DAY OF THE RITUAL

Burn Quimbanda Ritual Incense in the magical ritual area where you will be doing the ceremony.

Draw the Quimbanda spirit signature that represents the Seventh Lesser Quimbanda

Kingdom on the floor using red pemba (ritual chalk) directly in front of the altar of the Quimbanda Trinity deities.

Draw the Quimbanda spirit signature for Exu Rei Das Sete Praias on the floor using black pemba (ritual chalk) on the left side of the spirit signature that represents the Seventh Lesser Quimbanda Kingdom.

Draw the Quimbanda spirit signature for Pomba Gira Reina Das Sete Praias on the floor using white pemba (ritual chalk) on the left side of the spirit signature that represents the Seventh Lesser Quimbanda Kingdom.

Place a red candle on top of the spirit signature that represents the Seventh Lesser Quimbanda Kingdom.

Place a black candle on top of the spirit signature that represents Exu Rei Das Sete Praias.

Place a red candle on top of the spirit signature that represents Pomba Gira Reina Das Sete Praias.

Begin the Quimbanda ritual by lighting the red candle first, the black candle second and the white candle last.

While lighting the candles recite the following ritual prayers:

*IN THE NAME OF NZAMBI, THE GOD OF THE HEAVENS AND THE EARTH - SARAVA*
*IN THE NAME OF EXU MAIORAL - SARAVA*

*IN THE NAME OF EXU REI - SARAVA*
*IN THE NAME OF MARIA PADILLA REINA - SARAVA*
*IN THE NAME OF THE QUIMBANDA TRINITY - SARAVA*
*I, say your complete birth name, INVOKE YOUR SACRED AND DIVINE POWERS IN THE NAME OF DIVINE JUSTICE.*
*BY THE DIVINE POWER OF KING* ***EXU REI DAS SETE PRAIAS*** *& QUEEN* ***POMBA GIRA REINA DAS SETE PRAIAS*** *OF THE KINGDOM OF THE BEACHES, I DO INVOKE AND DO SUMMON THE GUARDIAN SPIRITS WHICH PROTECT THIS REALM AND GIVE LIFE TO THIS SACRED RITUAL. BY THE DIVINE SWORD KING EXU REI DAS SETE PRAIAS & QUEEN POMBA GIRA REINA DAS SETE PRAIAS, I DO SUMMON AND I DO COMMAND THE GUARDIAN SPIRITS OF THE REALM OF THE BEACHES IN THE NAME OF DIVINE JUSTICE TO DESTROY MY ENEMIES KNOWN AND UNKNOWN. I INVOKE THE POWERS OF THE QUIMBANDA CROSS TO COVER MY BODY IN PROTECTIVE LIGHT SO THAT MY ENEMIES KNOWN AND UNKNOW WILL NOT BE ABLE TO SEE NOR HEAR THIS SACRED RITUAL. I INVOKE AND SUMMON THE CHIEF SPIRIT,* ***EXU DOS RIOS****, TO BIND, BLIND, DESTROY AND CONQUER MY ENEMIES. O MOST GLORIOUS CHIEF SPIRIT, EXU DOS RIOS, MY ENEMIES ARE YOUR ENEMIES AND YOUR ENEMIES ARE MY ENEMIES. O MOST GLORIOUS CHIEF SPIRIT, EXU DOS RIOS, GUARDIAN OF THE REINO DA PRAIA, I LAY MY ENEMIES AT YOUR FEET. I INVOKE AND SUMMON THE CHIEF SPIRIT,* ***EXU DAS CACHOEIRAS****, TO BIND, BLIND, DESTROY AND CONQUER MY ENEMIES. O MOST GLORIOUS CHIEF SPIRIT, EXU DAS CACHOEIRAS, MY ENEMIES ARE YOUR ENEMIES AND YOUR ENEMIES ARE MY ENEMIES. O MOST GLORIOUS CHIEF SPIRIT, EXU DAS CACHOEIRAS, GUARDIAN OF THE REINO DA PRAIA, I LAY MY ENEMIES AT YOUR FEET. I INVOKE AND SUMMON THE CHIEF SPIRIT,* ***EXU DA PEDRA PRETA****, TO BIND, BLIND, DESTROY AND CONQUER MY ENEMIES. O MOST GLORIOUS CHIEF SPIRIT, EXU DA PEDRA PRETA, MY ENEMIES ARE YOUR ENEMIES AND YOUR ENEMIES ARE MY ENEMIES. MOST GLORIOUS CHIEF SPIRIT, EXU DA PEDRA PRETA, GUARDIAN OF THE REINO DA PRAIA, I LAY MY ENEMIES AT YOUR FEET. I INVOKE AND SUMMON THE CHIEF SPIRIT,* ***EXU MARINHEIRO****, TO BIND, BLIND, DESTROY AND CONQUER MY*

*ENEMIES. O MOST GLORIOUS CHIEF SPIRIT, EXU MARINHEIRO, MY ENEMIES ARE YOUR ENEMIES AND YOUR ENEMIES ARE MY ENEMIES. O MOST GLORIOUS CHIEF SPIRIT, EXU MARINHEIRO, GUARDIAN OF THE REINO DA PRAIA, I LAY MY ENEMIES AT YOUR FEET. I INVOKE AND SUMMON THE CHIEF SPIRIT,* ***EXU DO LODO****, TO BIND, BLIND, DESTROY AND CONQUER MY ENEMIES. O MOST GLORIOUS CHIEF SPIRIT, EXU DO LODO, MY ENEMIES ARE YOUR ENEMIES AND YOUR ENEMIES ARE MY ENEMIES. O MOST GLORIOUS CHIEF SPIRIT, EXU DO LODO, GUARDIAN OF THE REINO DA PRAIA, I LAY MY ENEMIES AT YOUR FEET. I INVOKE AND SUMMON THE CHIEF SPIRIT,* ***EXU MARE****, TO BIND, BLIND, DESTROY AND CONQUER MY ENEMIES. O MOST GLORIOUS CHIEF SPIRIT, EXU MARE, MY ENEMIES ARE YOUR ENEMIES AND YOUR ENEMIES ARE MY ENEMIES. O MOST GLORIOUS CHIEF SPIRIT, EXU MARE, GUARDIAN OF THE REINO DA PRAIA, I LAY MY ENEMIES AT YOUR FEET. I INVOKE AND SUMMON THE CHIEF SPIRIT,* ***EXU BAHIANO****, TO BIND, BLIND, DESTROY AND CONQUER MY ENEMIES. O MOST GLORIOUS CHIEF SPIRIT, EXU BAHIANO, MY ENEMIES ARE YOUR ENEMIES AND YOUR ENEMIES ARE MY ENEMIES. O MOST GLORIOUS CHIEF SPIRIT, EXU BAHIANO, GUARDIAN OF THE REINO DA PRAIA, I LAY MY ENEMIES AT YOUR FEET. I INVOKE AND SUMMON THE CHIEF SPIRIT,* ***EXU DOS VENTOS****, TO BIND, BLIND, DESTROY AND CONQUER MY ENEMIES. O MOST GLORIOUS CHIEF SPIRIT, EXU DOS VENTOS, MY ENEMIES ARE YOUR ENEMIES AND YOUR ENEMIES ARE MY ENEMIES. O MOST GLORIOUS CHIEF SPIRIT, EXU DOS VENTOS, GUARDIAN OF THE REINO DA PRAIA, I LAY MY ENEMIES AT YOUR FEET. I INVOKE AND SUMMON THE CHIEF SPIRIT,* ***EXU DO COCO****, TO BIND, BLIND, DESTROY AND CONQUER MY ENEMIES. O MOST GLORIOUS CHIEF SPIRIT, EXU DO COCO, MY ENEMIES ARE YOUR ENEMIES AND YOUR ENEMIES ARE MY ENEMIES. O MOST GLORIOUS CHIEF SPIRIT, EXU DO COCO, GUARDIAN OF THE REINO DA PRAIA, I LAY MY ENEMIES AT YOUR FEET. BY THE POWER AND THE VIRTUES OF THE GUARDIANS OF THE SACRED SEVEN QUIMBANDA KINGDOMS,* ***EXU DOS RIOS, EXU DAS CACHOEIRAS, EXU DA PEDRA PRETA, EXU MARINHEIRO, EXU DO LODO, EXU MARE, EXU BAHIANO,***

***EXU DOS VENTOS*** *AND* ***EXU DO COCO****, I DO SUMMON YOU HERE O POWERFUL QUIMBANDA SPIRITS AND COMMAND THIS RITUAL INTO BEING. IN THE NAME OF THE QUIMBANDA TRINITY AND LAWS OF DIVINE JUSTICE -* ***SARAVA***

*IN THE NAME OF NZAMBI, THE LORD OF HEAVEN - SARAVA. IN THE NAME OF THE QUIMBANDA TRINITY, WHO GOVERN THE HEAVENS AND THE EARTH - SARAVA. EXU BY THE DIVINE SWORD OF THE KING OF KINGS, I LAY MY ENEMIES AT YOUR FEET-SARAVA. EXU BY THE DIVINE SWORD OF THE KING OF KINGS, I DO BIND MY ENEMIES IN THY MOST SACRED NAME-SARAVA. EXU BY THE DIVINE SWORD OF THE KING OF KINGS, I DO BLIND MY ENEMIES IN THY MOST SACRED NAME-SARAVA. EXU BY THE DIVINE SWORD OF THE KING OF KINGS, I DO DESTROY MY ENEMIES IN THY MOST SACRED NAME-SARAVA. EXU BY THE DIVINE SWORD OF THE KING OF KINGS, I DO TRIUMPH OVER MY ENEMIES IN THY MOST SACRED NAME-SARAVA. EXU BY THE DIVINE SWORD OF THE KING OF KINGS, I DO CONQUEOR MY ENEMIES IN THY MOST SACRED NAME-SARAVA. EXU BY THE DIVINE SWORD OF THE KING OF KINGS, GRANT ME VICTORY OVER MY ENEMIES IN THY MOST SACRED NAME-SARAVA. EXU BY THE DIVINE SWORD OF THE KING OF KINGS AND BY THE DIVINE GRACE OF THE QUIMBANDA TRINITY AND THE SEVEN HOLY KINGDOMS, I LAY MY ENEMIES AT YOUR FEET. EXU BY THE DIVINE SWORD OF THE KING OF KINGS, I WASH MY HANDS CLEAN LIKE PONTIUS PILATE. EXU IN THE NAME OF DIVINE JUSTICE, GRANT MY REQUEST-SARAVA.*

*STATE YOUR REQUEST HERE & MEDITATE ON YOUR DESIRES*

## THE CONCLUDING RITUAL OF THE SEVENTH DAY

ALWAYS TAKE A QUIMBANDA CLEANSING BATH AT THE CONCLUSION OF EACH RITUAL.

*DO THE FOLLOWING RITUAL IF YOU DO NOT HAVE THE ACTUAL QUIMBANDA SPIRIT MYSTERIES:*

At the conclusion of the last of the seven day rituals take a spiritual offering to the crossroads for the Spirit Exu. The spiritual offering will include a bowl of roasted corn covered in palm oil (dende) and honey, an open bottle of Cachaça (Sugar Cane Liquor), 21 pennies, one lighted red candle, one lighted black candle, one lighted white candle and three lighted cigars.

*DO THE FOLLOWING RITUAL IF YOU HAVE THE ACTUAL QUIMBANDA NGANGA SPIRIT MYSTERIES:*

At the conclusion of the last of the seven day rituals do a traditional ritual blood offering to the Quimbanda spirits and then send them out with "Fula". After you have done this then wrap up the bodies of the three birds in black and red cloth along with roasted corn covered in palm oil (dende), honey and 21 pennies and leave it at a crossroads on top of a spirit signature (pontos riscados) of the spirit Exu Rei. Along with the bundle leave an open bottle of Cachaça, one lighted red candle, one lighted black candle, one lighted white candle and three lighted cigars.

## ALTERNATIVE SUGGESTIONS ABOUT HOW TO WIN A SPIRITUAL BATTLE AND DEFEAT YOUR ENEMIES

There are many ways to approach a spiritual battle. All of the following spiritual suggestions are recommended if you have been the constant target of witchcraft attacks by your enemies.

The first suggestion would be to get baptized into the mysteries of the Quimbanda Spirits. In the Quimbanda religious tradition, baptism is known by the Congo word, "**MASSANGUÀ**".

The second suggestion would be to become a full member of the Quimbanda religion by receiving a permanent spiritual protection known as "Scratching" or the Rayamento initiation ceremony. In the Quimbanda religious tradition, baptism is known by the Congo word, "**MUKASO**".

The third suggestion would be to receive the actual spiritual mysteries of the Quimbanda Trinity.

The fourth suggestion would be to have a powerful cleansing ceremony done by a Quimbanda Priest.

The fifth suggestion would be to have a ritual done to give spiritual offerings for the Quimbanda Spirits.

The sixth suggestion would be to have a set of ritual consecrated Quimbanda beads for made and presented to you of your father Exu and your mother Pomba Gira. Your spiritual mother and father can be determined through a divination done by an experienced Quimbandeiro Priest.

## THE QUIMBANDA SPIRIT METAL TOOLS (FERRAMENTAS)

**Ferramentas** are made of metal. The metal of choice is usually iron. The Ferramentas are metal tools of the Quimbanda spirits that represent their sacred spirit signature symbols. Each of the Quimbanda spirits has one that is unique and sacred to each one of them. Ferramentas are usually placed into the spirit ngangas or placed on Quimbanda altars to represent the spirits. Ferramentas can also be consecrated and empowered by a Quimbanda Priest by performing a sacred ritual to the spirits. Consecrated Ferramentas can be kept by both initiated and non-initiated members of the Quimbanda religion. Consecrated Ferramentas can be used to protect your home or business from spiritual attacks.

*A DIAGRAM PICTURE SHOWING THE FERRAMENTA OF KING EXU MAIORAL.*

## THE QUIMBANDA SPIRIT SIGNATURES (PONTOS RISCADOS)

In the Quimbanda magico-religious tradition, spirit signature sigils (seals) are symbols connected to a set of ideas by which spirits or deities may be summoned to awareness and controlled. The spirit signature sigils connect the spirits to our earthly realm. In the Portuguese language they are called "**Pontos Riscados**". The spirit signature sigils when used in the appropriate magical manner open up the doors to world of the supernatural. They are used in divinatory practices. The spirit signature sigil itself when drawn out on the ground or drawn on an object will call forth the spirit. The spirit signature sigil also serves as a physical focus through which the Quimbanda Priest achieves the desired state of mind. Spirit signature sigils represent the secret names of spirits and deities who manifest themselves differently to each magic practitioner. Once the Quimbanda Priest has summoned the spirit or deity he may control it, if necessary, by subjecting its sigil to fire or the use of a magical sword or machete. Spirit signature sigils can also serve as amulets, talismans, or meditation tools. Quimbanda spirit signature sigils may be of various signs, such as crosses, tridents, stars associated with different deities. Quimbanda Priests often times inscribe the spirit signature sigil on ceremonial ritual objects, candles or objects of silver, brass, gold, or glass. Such spirit signatures sigils are considered to be magically powerful. Quimbanda Priests also draw these very sacred and powerful spirit signature sigils directly on the ground in front of the spirit ngangas of the Quimbanda Spirits to invoke and to summon the deities to appear and to send them to do their bidding. The following Quimbanda spirit signature sigils (Pontos Riscados) can be used when doing the Quimbanda magical spells and rituals from this book and when making a spirit nganga, amulets, mojo bags, macutos and candles.

*A DIAGRAM SHOWING THE SACRED SPIRIT SIGNATURE OF THE QUIMBANDA TRINITY (QUIMBANDA CROSS).*

*A DIAGRAM SHOWING THE SACRED SPIRIT SIGNATURE OF EXU MAIORAL.*

*A DIAGRAM SHOWING THE SACRED SPIRIT SIGNATURE OF EXU REI.*

*A DIAGRAM SHOWING THE SACRED SPIRIT SIGNATURE OF MARIA PADILLA REINA.*

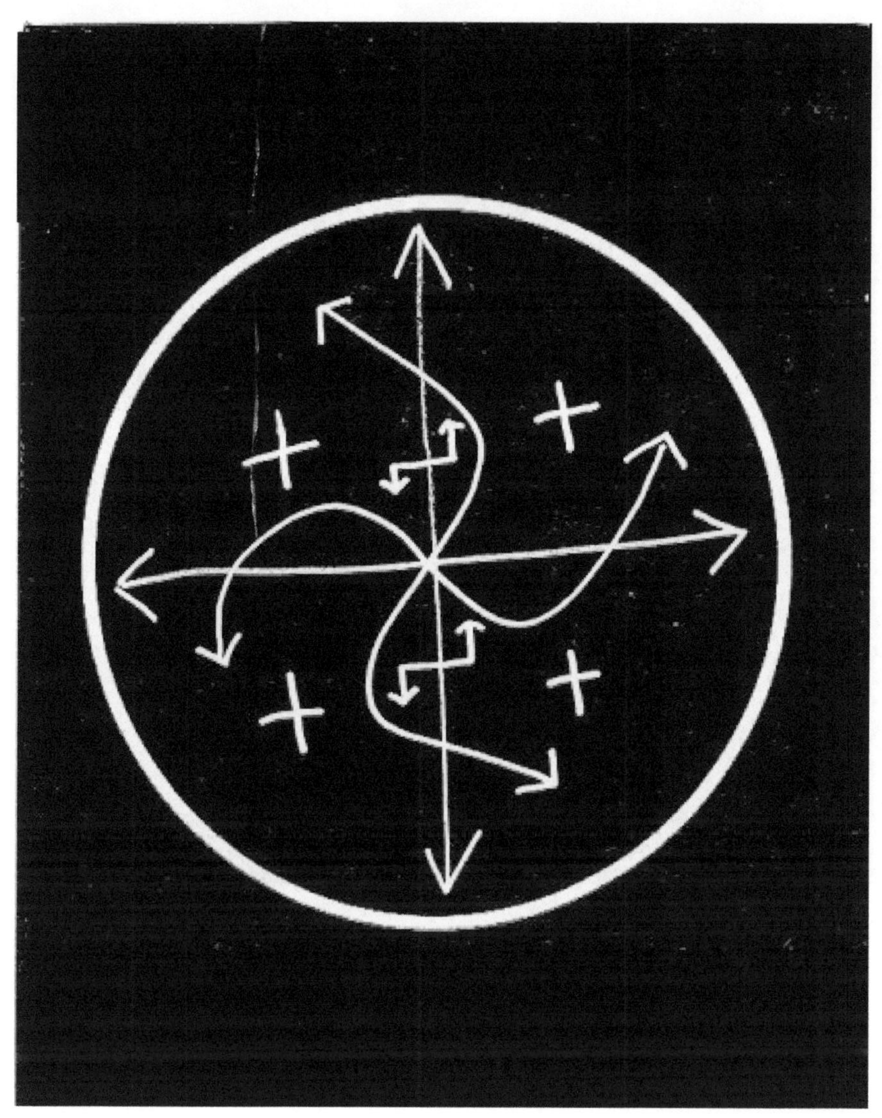

*A DIAGRAM SHOWING THE SACRED SPIRIT SIGNATURE OF MUKOMBE (SAINT GEORGE).*

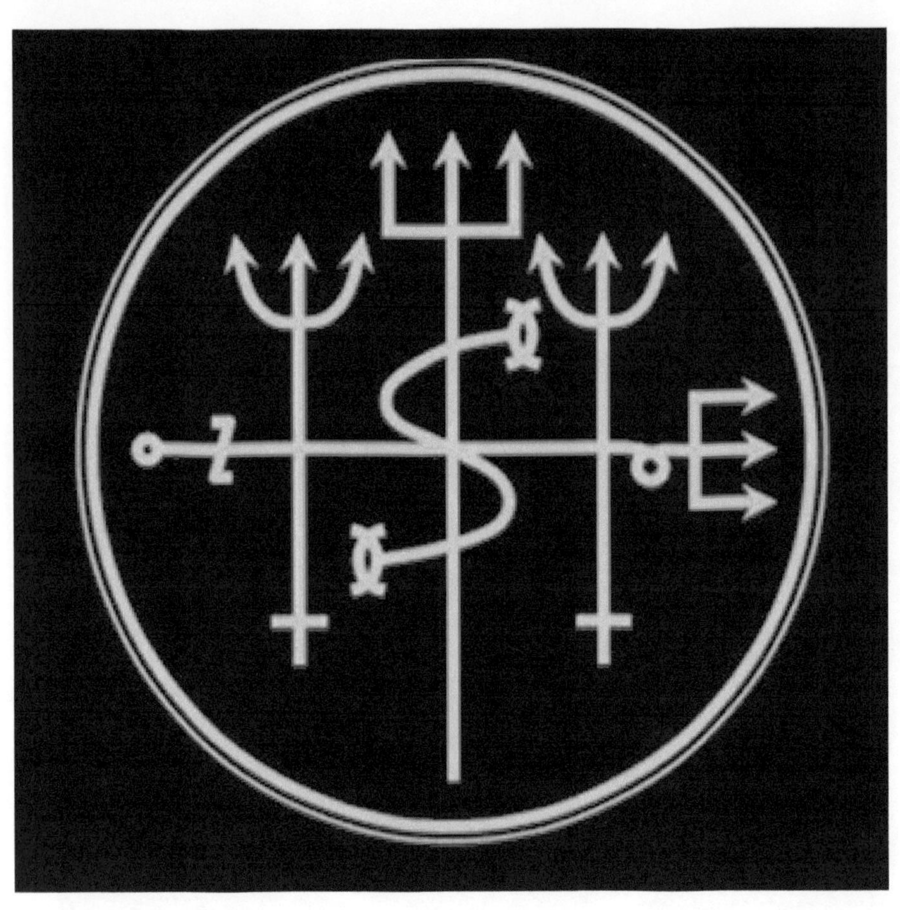

*A DIAGRAM SHOWING THE SACRED SPIRIT SIGNATURE OF EXU MEIA NOITE.*

*A DIAGRAM SHOWING THE SACRED SPIRIT SIGNATURE OF THE FIRST KINGDOM: KINGDOM THE CROSSROADS (REINO DAS ENCRUZILHADAS).*

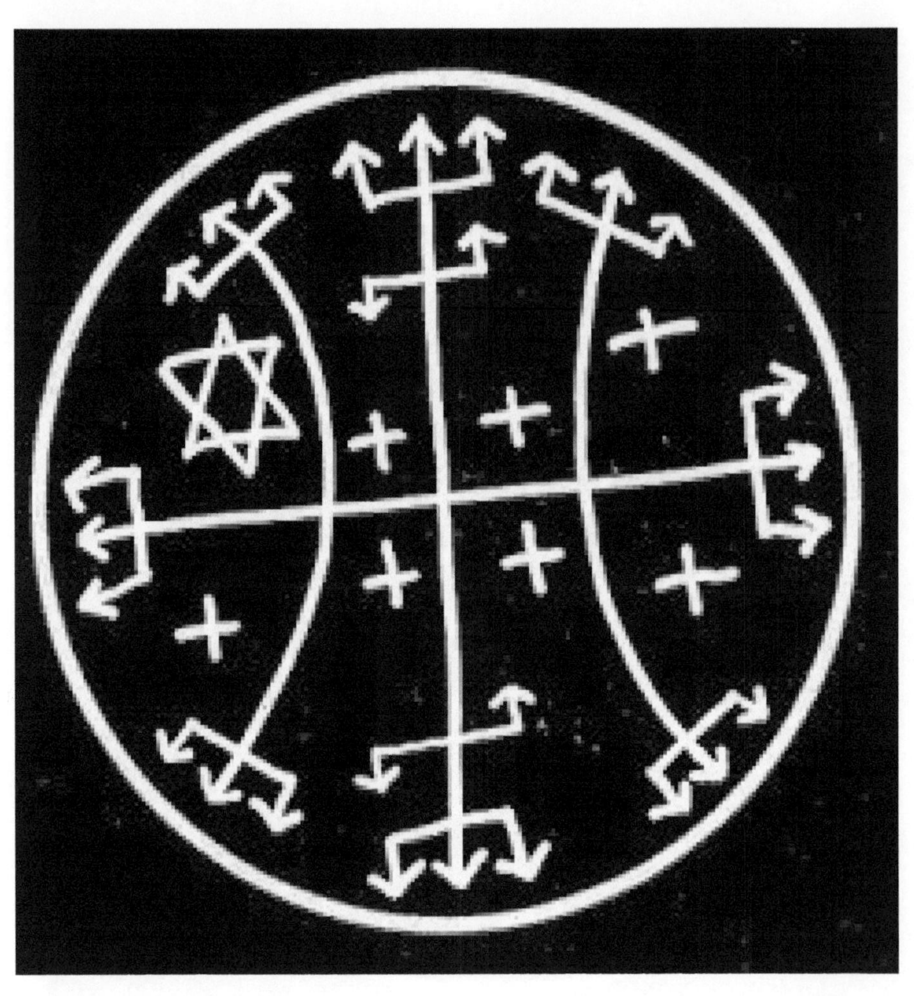

*A DIAGRAM SHOWING THE SACRED SPIRIT SIGNATURE OF KING EXU REI DAS ENCRUZILHADAS.*

*A DIAGRAM SHOWING THE SACRED SPIRIT SIGNATURE OF QUEEN POMBA GIRA REINA DAS ENCRUZILHADAS.*

*A DIAGRAM SHOWING THE SACRED SPIRIT SIGNATURE OF THE SECOND KINGDOM: KINGDOM OF THE CROSSINGS (REINO DOS CRUZEIROS).*

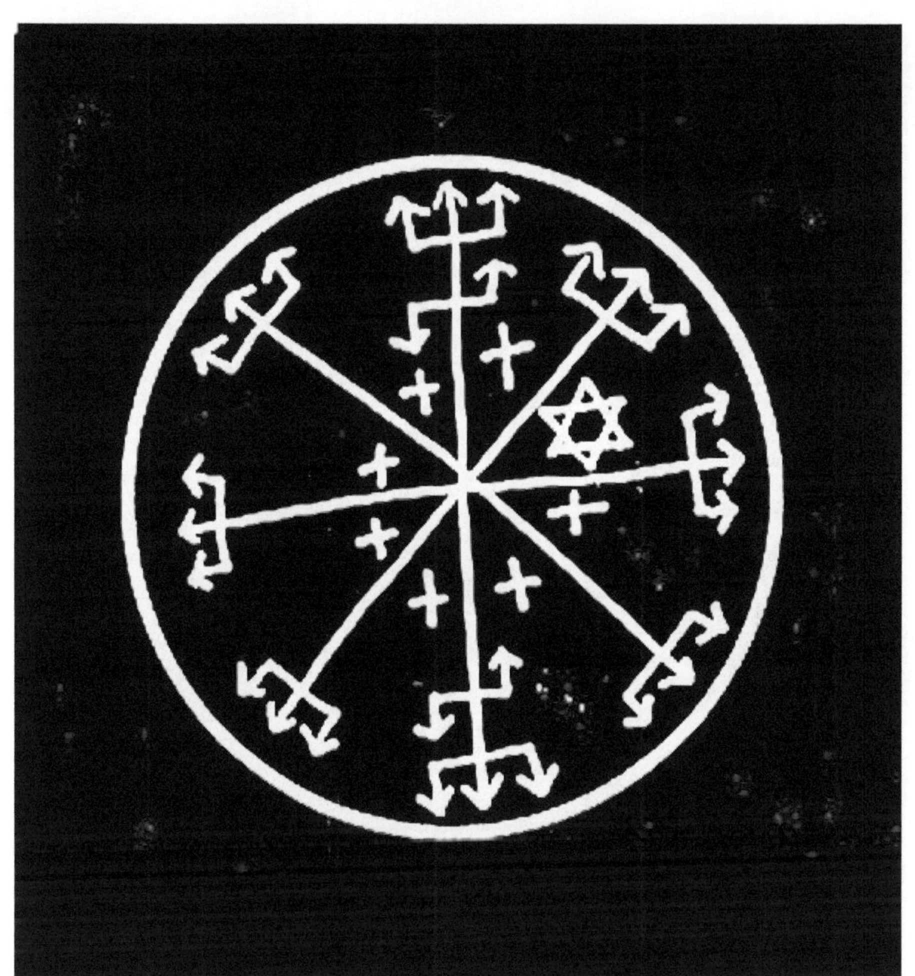

*A DIAGRAM SHOWING THE SACRED SPIRIT SIGNATURE OF KING EXU REI DOS 7 CRUZEIROS.*

*A DIAGRAM SHOWING THE SACRED SPIRIT SIGNATURE OF QUEEN POMBA GIRA REINA DOS 7 CRUZEIROS.*

*DIAGRAM SHOWING THE SACRED SPIRIT SIGNATURE OF THE THIRD KINGDOM: KINGDOM OF THE MOUNTAINS & FOREST (REINO DAS MATAS).*

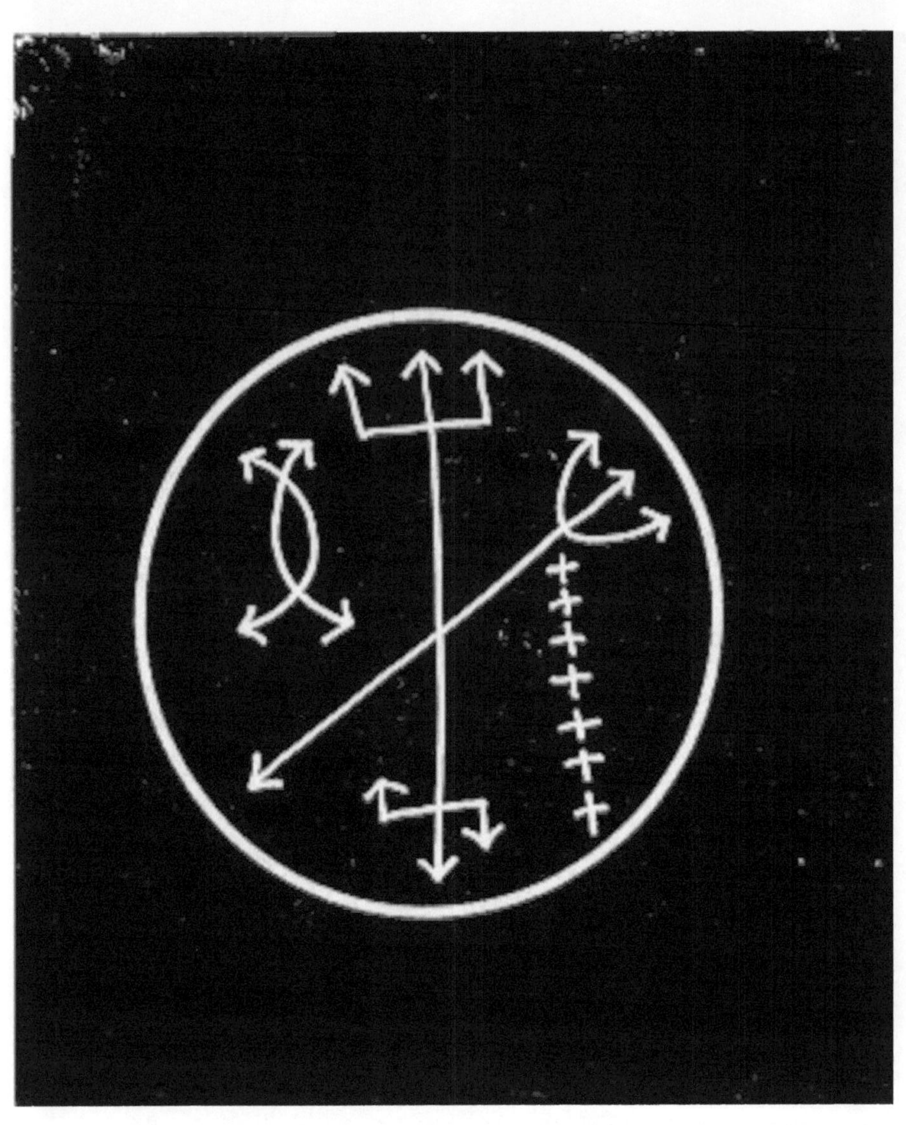

*A DIAGRAM SHOWING THE SACRED SPIRIT SIGNATURE OF KING EXU REI DAS MATAS.*

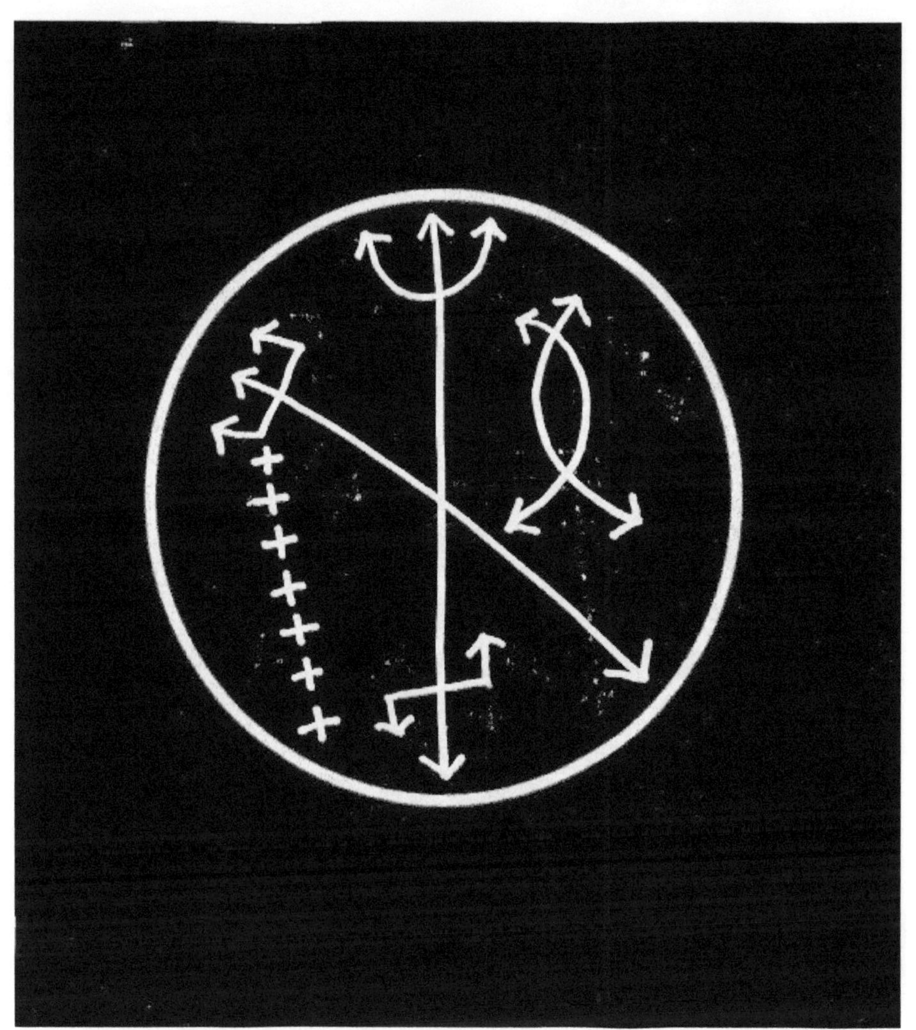

*A DIAGRAM SHOWING THE SACRED SPIRIT SIGNATURE OF QUEEN POMBA GIRA REINA DAS MATAS.*

*A DIAGRAM SHOWING THE SACRED SPIRIT SIGNATURE OF THE FOURTH KINGDOM: KINGDOM OF THE CEMETERY (REINO DA KALUNGA).*

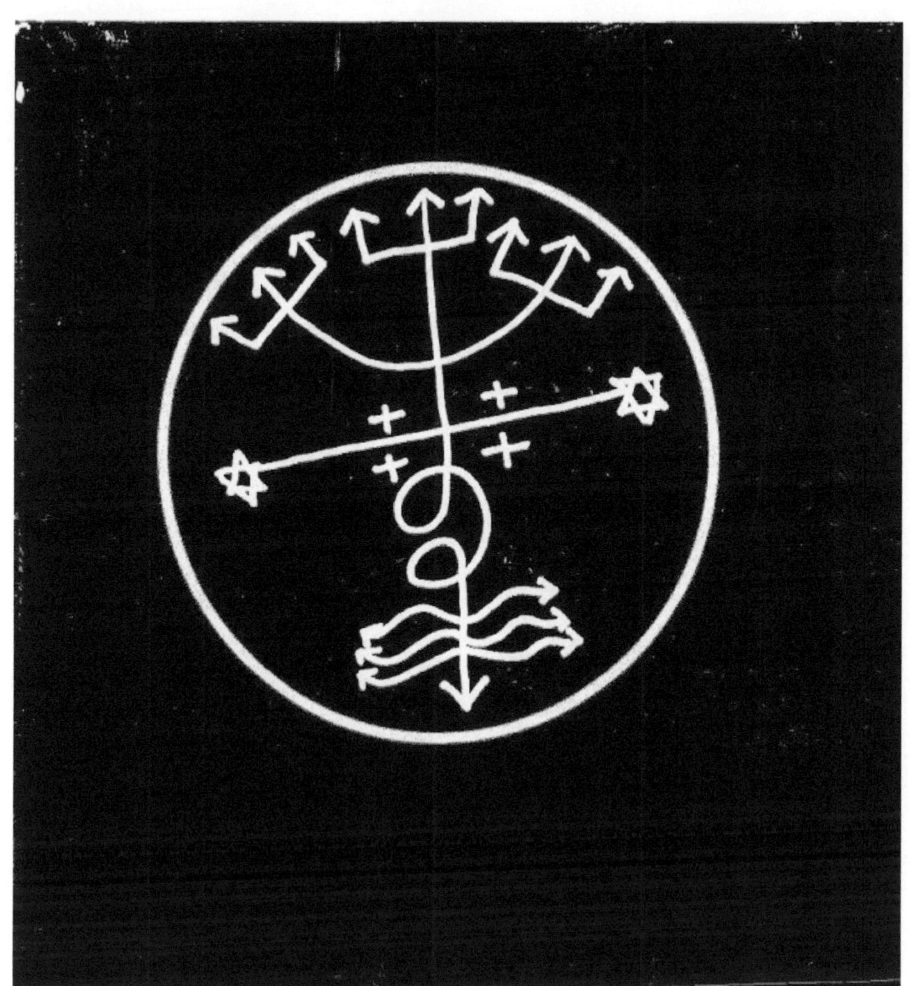

*A DIAGRAM SHOWING THE SACRED SPIRIT SIGNATURE OF KING EXU REI KALUNGA.*

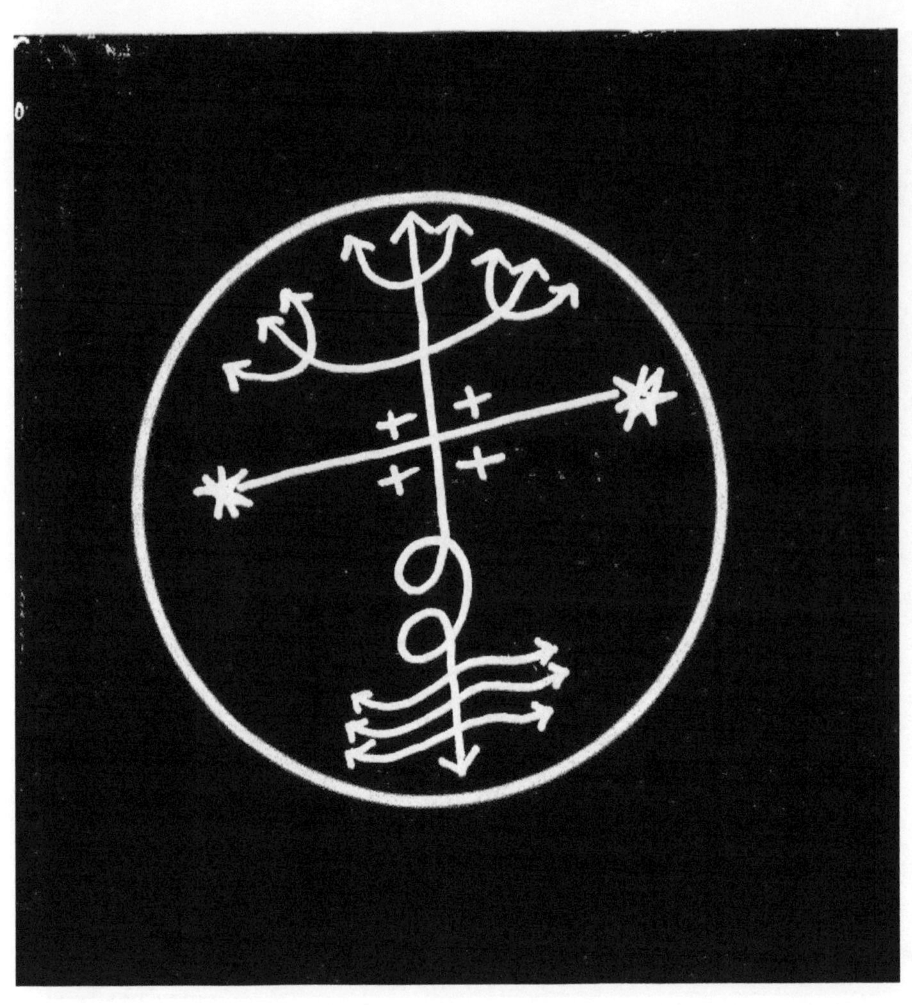

*A DIAGRAM SHOWING THE SACRED SPIRIT SIGNATURE OF QUEEN POMBA GIRA REINA KALUNGA.*

*A DIAGRAM SHOWING THE SACRED SPIRIT SIGNATURE OF THE FIFTH KINGDOM: KINGDOM OF THE SOULS (REINO DAS ALMAS).*

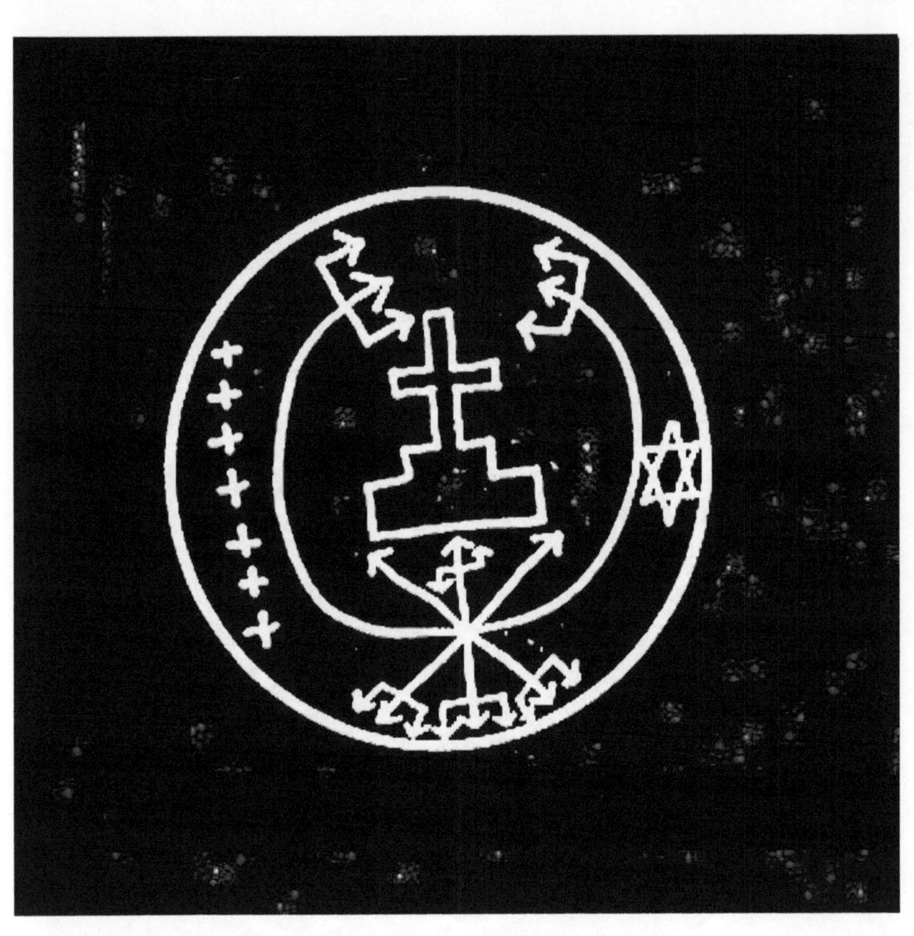

*A DIAGRAM SHOWING THE SACRED SPIRIT SIGNATURE OF KING EXU REI DAS ALMAS.*

*A DIAGRAM SHOWING THE SACRED SPIRIT SIGNATURE OF QUEEN POMBA GIRA REINA DAS ALMAS.*

*A DIAGRAM SHOWING THE SACRED SPIRIT SIGNATURE OF THE SIXTH KINGDOM: KINGDOM OF THE LYRE (REINO DAS LIRAS).*

*A DIAGRAM SHOWING THE SACRED SPIRIT SIGNATURE OF KING EXU REI DAS LIRAS.*

*A DIAGRAM SHOWING THE SACRED SPIRIT SIGNATURE OF QUEEN POMBA GIRA REINA DAS LIRAS.*

*DIAGRAM SHOWING THE SACRED SPIRIT SIGNATURE OF THE SEVENTH KINGDOM: KINGDOM OF THE BEACH (REINO DA PRAIA).*

*A DIAGRAM SHOWING THE SACRED SPIRIT SIGNATURE OF KING EXU REI DAS SETE PRAIAS.*

*A DIAGRAM SHOWING THE SACRED SPIRIT SIGNATURE OF QUEEN POMBA GIRA REINA DAS SETE PRAIAS.*

www.ingramcontent.com/pod-product-compliance
Ingram Content Group UK Ltd.
Pitfield, Milton Keynes, MK11 3LW, UK
UKHW041929190726
13854UKWH00004B/1522

9 781105 803697